A Nouthetic Approach To Healing Posttraumatic Stress Disorder

By Angie Fried

Edited by JC Madison

ISBN: 0615537847
ISBN-13: 9780615537849

Dedication

To those who are suffering with PTSD and for those who lend their love and support to them,

To Dr. Meghan Birt who introduced me to the Emotion Code and all of the resultant healing that has come from mastering it,

And to Karen Hime who conceived of this endeavor in the first place and asked me to write the book.

For George Johnson - may the Lord Himself bless you in your endeavors as you reach out to serve & heal veterans

Table of Contents

Introduction

This book is for those who are suffering with PTSD. This suffering takes many forms. But this book is also for people who are close to them, and anyone who is genuinely endeavoring to treat people suffering with PTSD. It is for our society, and even for our global community because PTSD is a humanity-wide issue. PTSD does not know any boundaries; people of every class, country, religion, age, sex and language are affected by PTSD. This book is for anyone and everyone, whether you are simply trying to understand PTSD or trying to live with it in some capacity.

This book will be facing the suffering of PTSD throughout. Yet I intend to offer hope to those who suffer as I do. God heals. The redemptive nature of salvation through faith in the person and finished work of Christ offers healing of many kinds. While it takes time, God does offer and even promise to restore us as we work through our trials and hurts with faith in His purposes. But the way in which we look at our lives (and I know this from personal experience) will enable us to take advantage of our spiritual resources, or rob us of them. The strength, wisdom, freedom and hope that Christ offers us only comes through grasping that He does not promise us a restoration of our former way of life, before our PTSD or the events precipitating PTSD, but He wants to restore us from our brokenness and use it to make us like His Son. This is His purpose in all suffering.

What will matter most to our success in this challenge is our perspective on what God is doing. We must have an eternal focus. This is a focus that respects God's overall agenda in creation (to glorify Himself) and His purpose for our lives (our conformity to the image of His Son, Christ). Apart from the saving knowledge of Christ and hence the subsequent indwelling of the Holy Spirit, we will never be able to tap into these purposes. God's redemptive work in our lives begins the moment that we put our faith in the person of Jesus Christ (He is the Son of God, just as He said) and the work that He accomplished on the cross at Calvary (His death, burial and resurrection, 1 Corinthians 15:3,4). From the moment of salvation forward, He continues to work and to accomplish His will in our lives for His good pleasure. Our growth will be in good measure dependent upon our cooperation with Him in this process i.e., we need to be faithful in reading the Word of God daily, studying it, memorizing it, attending a Bible-believing and preaching church and being obedient to the revealed will of God as taught in Scripture. If we shift our focus to things of the earth, our problems, circumstances, family, etc. then we will begin to be defeated in that moment. We must faithfully pursue the knowledge of the Holy One in our lives to be transformed from the inside out.

Much of this book is dependent upon this transformational truth. If you refuse to acknowledge God or believe in Him, if you are angry with Him or bitter with Him and shake your fist at heaven, then many of the truths included will be of little use to you. But you are only hindering your own healing, not hurting God. However, He wants to give you the abundant life, which can only come with a right response to suffering. It is my hope that this book will help equip people with the basics needed to get started on a journey of healing.

The principles in this book are intended to help anyone facing their own mountain. They are timeless principles. It is my hope that people will not just learn how to overcome the issues of PTSD, but it is also my hope that they will learn a blueprint of how to overcome, period.

If you do not know Christ as your Savior please take the time right now to bow your head and simply ask Him to forgive you of your sins and give you eternal life. If you believe in your heart that God raised Him from the dead and you confess with your mouth that Jesus Christ is Lord then you shall be saved. This book and its answers will become much more meaningful and relevant to you as you face the hurdles that are crippling people's lives, possibly including your own. The power to live the victorious, overcomers' life is found in Christ and Christ alone. Will you receive that gift now?

Sample prayer:

Dear Jesus, I know I am a sinner and that I need forgiveness for my sins. I ask you now, believing that You will honor Your Word and forgive me my sins, to grant me that saving forgiveness and give me eternal life with you when I die. Begin to change and transform me into the image of my Savior. Please use the information in these pages to aid that process. Amen.

We live in a world where bad things happen every day to millions of people. God the Father freely offers us the best gift of all: the Spirit of God, the Spirit of Christ, to go with us in all circumstances and at all times. We can have that relationship, and it leads to an eternal relationship. In a world where relationships end, where they fail us and we fail in them, it is encouraging to know that He will never leave us or forsake us.

Nothing in this world can separate us from the love of God - not trouble, distress, hardship, PTSD or anything else in all of creation (Romans 8:35). The love of God through Jesus Christ will keep us safe. It is yours for the asking. All who genuinely seek Him in truth, find Him.

What is Posttraumatic Stress Disorder (PTSD)?

Posttraumatic Stress Disorder (PTSD) is an anxiety disorder that can occur after you have been through a traumatic event. A traumatic event[1] is something horrible and frightening that you see or that happens to you. During this type of event, you think that your life or others' lives are in danger. You may feel afraid or feel that you have no control over what is happening.

Anyone who has gone through a life-threatening event can develop PTSD. These events can include:

Combat or military exposure
Child sexual or physical abuse
Terrorist attacks

---

1 The definition of traumatic is as follows: 1. A serious injury or shock to the body, as from violence or an accident. 2. An emotional wound or shock that creates substantial, lasting damage to the psychological development of a person, often leading to neurosis. 3. An event or situation that causes great distress and disruption. This information was provided from http://www.thefreedictionary.com/traumatic.

Sexual or physical assault

Serious accidents, such as a car wreck.

Natural disasters, such as a fire, tornado, hurricane, flood, or earthquake

After the event, you may feel scared, confused or angry. If these feelings don't go away or they get worse, you may have PTSD. These symptoms may disrupt your life, making it hard to continue with your normal activities.

How does PTSD develop?

All people with PTSD have lived through a traumatic event that has caused them to fear for their lives, see horrible things, and feel helpless. Strong emotions caused by the event create changes in the brain that may result in PTSD.

Most people who go through a traumatic event have a number symptoms of PTSD at the beginning, though only some will develop PTSD. It isn't clear why some people develop PTSD and others don't. The likeliness of developing PTSD depends on many things. These include:

The intensity of the traumas or its duration

If you lost someone you were close to or if you or they were hurt

How close you were to the event

How strong your reaction was

How much you felt in control of events

How much help and support you got after the event

Many people who develop PTSD get better at some time, but about 1 out of 3 people with PTSD may continue to have some symptoms. Even if you continue to have symptoms, treatment can help you cope. Your symptoms do not have to interfere with your everyday activities, work, and relationships.

What are the symptoms of PTSD?

Symptoms of posttraumatic stress disorder (PTSD) can be terrifying. They may disrupt your life and make it hard to continue with your daily activities. It may be hard just to get through the day.

PTSD symptoms usually start soon after the traumatic event, but they may not happen until months or years later. They also may come and go over many years. If the symptoms last longer than 4 weeks, cause you great distress, or interfere with your work or home life, you might have PTSD.
There are four types of symptoms: reliving the event, avoidance, numbness, and feeling keyed up.

Reliving the event (also called re-experiencing symptoms):

Bad memories of the traumatic event can come back at any time. You may feel the same fear and horror you did when the event took place. You may have nightmares. You may have daymares. You even may feel like you're going through the event again.

This is called a flashback. Sometimes there is a trigger - a sound or sight that causes you to relive the event. Triggers might include:

> Hearing a car backfire, which can bring back memories of gunfire and war for a combat veteran
> Seeing a car accident, which can remind a crash survivor of his or her own accident
> Seeing a news report of a sexual assault, which may bring back memories of assault for a woman who was raped

Avoiding situations that remind you of the event:

You may try to avoid situations or people that trigger memories of the traumatic event. You may even avoid talking or thinking about the event.

> A person who was in an earthquake may avoid watching television shows or movies in which there are earthquakes
> A person who was robbed at gunpoint while ordering at a hamburger drive-in may avoid fast-food restaurants
> Some people may keep very busy or avoid seeking help. This keeps them from having to think or talk about the event

Feeling numb:

You may find it hard to express your feelings. This is another way to avoid memories.

You may not have positive or loving feelings toward other
people and may avoid relationships

You may not be interested in activities you used to enjoy

You may forget about parts of the traumatic event or not be
able to talk about them.

Feeling keyed up (also called hyperarousal):

You may be jittery, or always alert and on the lookout for danger.
This is known as hyperarousal. It can feel like you are constantly
adrenalated. It can cause you to:

Suddenly become angry or irritable

Have a hard time sleeping

Have trouble concentrating

Fear for your safety and always feel on guard

Be very startled when someone surprises you

What are other common problems?

People with PTSD may also have other problems. These include:

Drinking or drug problems

Feelings of hopelessness, shame, or despair

Employment problems

Relationship problems including divorce and violence

Physical symptoms

Can children have PTSD?

Children can have PTSD too. They may have the symptoms described above or other symptoms depending upon their age. As children get older their symptoms are more like those of adults.

Young children may become upset if their parents are not close by, have trouble sleeping, or suddenly have trouble with toilet training or going to the bathroom

Children who are in the first few years of elementary school (ages 6 to 9) may act out the trauma through play, drawings, or stories. They may complain of physical problems or become more irritable or aggressive. They also may develop fears and anxiety that don't seem to be caused by the traumatic event.

What treatments are available?

When you have PTSD, dealing with the past can be hard. Instead of telling others how you feel, you may keep your feelings bottled up.

The secular world offers treatment for PTSD. Cognitive-behavioral therapy (CBT) is one type of counseling. It appears to be the most commonly used type of counseling for PTSD in the medical and secular world. There are different types of cognitive behavioral therapies such as cognitive therapy and exposure therapy.

A similar kind of therapy called EMDR, or eye movement desensitization and reprocessing, is also used for PTSD. Medications can be used as well. A type of drug known as a selective sero-tonin reuptake inhibitor (SSRI), which is also used for depres-sion, can offer some temporary relief for PTSD.

However, it should be noted that newer possibilities exist. If a person is open to trying something that is presently considered "unconventional" s/he may find greater relief. I am speaking of Dr. Bradley Nelson's work in the field of emotional release. He has written a book entitled, *The Emotion Code,* wherein he dis-cusses how to release trapped emotions in order for us to be free from them.

I CANNOT RECOMMEND THIS BOOK HIGHLY ENOUGH! I was first exposed to it through the chiroprac-tor's office and learned the basics from them. After reading the book I have been using this method to process out a life-time of traumatic events and the emotional baggage that they have encumbered me with. ***This has been dramatically more effec-tive for overcoming issues of trauma than any other method that I have used***. While there are other things that one can use in tandem, this alone has been monumentally helpful to me!

Dr. Nelson has offered this book to soldiers free of charge on line at TheEmotionCode.com/SaveaSoldier. Every veteran needs to use this resource to become free from the life-dominating issues involved in having PTSD.

Having said that, I will move on to the other issues involved in counseling those with PTSD.

What is Nouthetic Counseling?

Nouthetic counseling comes from the Greek and is an elastic word meaning to speak to the need of the moment. Sometimes people need encouragement, sometimes they need a reprimand, sometimes they need silence or just information that was lacking. While this does not sound all that revolutionary, we often have people say things that are not helpful but are actually hurtful to us in the midst of our traumas or trials. And sometimes it is merely the manner in which they speak or the judgments that are cast upon us.

Nouthetesos is the word used in Scripture, the Bible, to address this issue of speaking to the need of the moment. It is necessary to have the boldness, the honesty and the gentleness to say what needs to be said to those who come for counseling. Wisdom in what is said and how it is said is crucial to the healing power of our words.

But where does the wisdom come from? The best and primary source is the Bible. Nouthetic counselors use the Scripture to counsel people, to lead them out of the bondage of wrong thinking and hence wrong living. Our emotions follow our actions, which follow our thoughts. Put simply: right thinking leads to right living. And our emotions follow those two like the tail on a dog. To purify what we emote, we must change the way that we think.

And what do we change to? Truth. Specifically, Biblical truth. Christ came to set us free so we can live our lives to our fullest potential and the truth will set us free. If our thinking is not righteous by Biblical standards then our living will not be righteous either; if the source of our philosophy is polluted then our lives are going to be polluted.

Stated plainly: <u>*not all sources of so-called truth are equal and therefore the conclusion can only be that not all "truth" is equally good, useful or valid for living out our lives to our fullest potential and the glory of God!*</u>

Ultimately, what I am saying is that we need the purest form of truth available to live our lives to our fullest. That means Biblical truth must inform our every day lives and our decisions about everything.

This having been said, it is necessary to note that Biblical ignorance has skyrocketed in recent decades, even within the church itself. People simply do not know how to apply the Word of God to their everyday problems and thus conclude that it is not relevant to every day issues. Nothing could be further from the truth!

Having received a bachelors in psychology from the College of Saint Benedict and later receiving training from Central Baptist

Theological Seminary in Biblical counseling I can readily con-
cede the superior nature of Biblical counseling to solve life's
most pressing problems.

How do you get started with Nouthetic Counseling?

The first thing to do is find someone who is certified by the
National Association of Nouthetic Counselors (NANC). Their
website is www.nanc.org.

It is also possible to find pastors who have graduated from
NANC-affiliated seminaries and who will help you begin estab-
lishing your thoughts in unadulterated truth. But beware! Not
everything we learn about how we think is easy to take. Our
thinking reveals our hearts - our very person. This is not always
pretty nor is it always easy. When we see ourselves for who we
are, we often get angry or defensive. This is common but not
useful for personal growth.

Rest assured that everyone, including your counselor(s), will be
in need of personal growth and therefore change as long as we
breathe air. Therefore, do not be discouraged by the scope and
depth of change that will be necessary to be victorious over your
battles. Rather, be confident that in Christ, with the right professional help, victory is indeed possible. All things are possible
with God (Luke 1:37).

Questions & Answers About Suffering

One of the deepest sorrows of our hearts is when we are so very troubled about suffering. More times than can ever be reckoned through human history people have asked, "Why does a good God allow or cause suffering?" The answer to this question, if wrong, can propel people away from God - sometimes for a lifetime. But if we can find the answers of faith to the age-old questions that plague us, we can find deep meaning and comfort in our suffering. Yes, comfort in the knowledge of a God that allows suffering - even great suffering. It is seen and recorded throughout Scripture and throughout history. Let us, therefore, examine this issue.

Below is a reprinted chapter from Elyse Fitzpatrick and Laura Hendrickson's book, *Will Medicine Stop the Pain?* It is chapter three in their book and that I have included here in its entirety because I simply cannot improve upon what they have said.

Lord, Why Do You Let Me Hurt?

Why are you in despair, O my soul? . . . Hope in
God, for I shall again praise Him.
Psalm 42:5

Up till now, you may have thought about your emotional pain as something that didn't really have much to do with your faith. It was just a dysfunction in the wiring or chemicals in your brain and didn't really involve your understanding of God, His plans, or his power. In some ways, viewing emotional pain as a materialist can be more comforting (at least on the surface) than the belief that God is sovereignly ruling over how you're feeling and that He is using your feelings for His purposes. But by now we can see that our emotions were given to us by God, and that it's His purpose to use them in our lives. How does that make you feel? We can imagine that right now your heart may be vacillating between two conflicting emotions: fear and hope.

The Fear of Change

Learning to think about life in a new way can be daunting. We all have favorite ways of comforting ourselves, dealing with our problems with familiar strategies, and of looking at our difficulties. Given enough time, we may learn to live with our pain. Though such coping may not be effective, because we're familiar with it, we are reluctant to try alternate solutions such as those found in the Bible. In fact, perhaps the mere thought that God is at work in our emotions makes you want to run and hide. You may feel as though you are being put on trial, or exposing yourself to just another opportunity to fail.

We also recognize that the thought of having to do the hard work of pursuing change can be discouraging. Please let us encourage you in this chapter (and in the ones to follow) that you really can have hope. God has led you here, to this book, at this time, and we know that He will use it in your life for His good purposes. God hasn't deserted you in your pain. *His plans for you are good.* In fact, one Puritan writer said, "[God] will use you only in safe and honorable services, and to no worse an end, than your endless happiness." He really is interested in your happiness, dear reader. But sometimes (as you're discovering) the road to happiness and joy frequently leads us through the valley of the shadow of death. We've both walked down that road, we've heard noises in the shadow and seen sights that have threatened to terrify us. But we've also learned that God will stay with us the whole way through. We've learned to say:

> Even through I walk through the valley of the shadow of death, I fear no evil, for You are with me; Your rod and Your staff, they comfort me. You prepare a table before me in the presence of my enemies; You have anointed my head with oil; my cup overflows. Surely goodness and lovingkindness will follow me all the days of my life, and I will dwell in the house of the Lord forever. (Psalm 23:4-6)

What benefits can you know in the midst of your pain? Right now, as you read this, God is with you. The knowledge that He is with you and will guide you can bring wonderful comfort. *You don't need to fear.* He's going to feed you, anoint you, and superabundantly bless you - right in the midst of your pain. He has surrounded you with His goodness and lovingkindness, and when He's finished with the work He's planned for you here on earth, you can be assured that His mighty power will be strong enough to bring you home to Himself. And you will dwell with Him *forever!* It's because of these truths that we can tell you not to be afraid. You don't even need to trust in your own ability to carry on in the fight. Trust in God and rest in His mighty hand. He will do His work; He will bring you to a place of endless happiness and peace - and all for His glory.

The Hope for Change

Although this new way of looking at your problems may be making you uncomfortable, it's probably also filling you with some glimmers of hope. Perhaps you're beginning to see that you won't have to think about yourself as a person who has some strange and incurable physiological problem that will continue for the rest of your life. Perhaps you're seeing that there really is hope for you and that you're not all that different from many others. Perhaps as you've considered what we've had to say, you're experiencing a growth of faith in your heart. You might be thinking, *You mean I don't have to live like this? You mean I can be more like other Christians?* We hope that's where you are, but even if it isn't, don't worry or be afraid. Remember that God is with you, and He is committed to using the resources of heaven to help you.

All God's Children Can Change

If there's one truth that Bible makes vividly clear, it's that we all can change. In fact, the Bible is the story of how God works in his children's lives to make them like Jesus Christ, the Son he loves. Everywhere we look in Scripture, we see encouragements to trust God, the atoning death of the Son, the power of the Spirit, the truth of His Word, and the strength of the church, His family. Think about the people whom God changed for His glory:

> He changed Abraham from a lying idolater into the "father of our faith."
> He changed Jacob, the scheming supplanted, into Israel, a prince with God.
> He changed Rahab from a harlot into a faithful woman, ancestor of King David and Jesus Christ.
> He changed Saul, the self-righteous persecutor of Christians, into Paul, the apostle to the Gentiles.
> He changed peter from a fearful people-pleaser into a faith-filled martyr.

If God was able to bring about dramatic changes in all those people, fallen people like us, then He is able to change you too. This is how Paul put it in 1 Corinthians 6:

> Do you not know that the unrighteous will not inherit the kingdom of God? Do not be deceived. Neither fornicators, nor idolaters, nor adulterers, nor homosexuals, nor sodomites, nor thieves, nor covetous, nor drunkards, nor revilers, nor

extortioners will inherit the kingdom of God. *And such were some of you.* But you were washed, but you were sanctified, but you were justified in the name of the Lord Jesus and by the Spirit of our God. (1 Corinthians 6.9-11, emphasis added)

Look again at the list of people above. Surely, if God was able to change them through His justifying and sanctifying power, He's able to change us, too. His power hasn't diminished, nor have His purposes varied. He's still in the business of conforming us to be more and more like His Son. So why not stop right now and pray? Thank God that He's making His truth and power known to you. Ask Him to help you believe that He can work in your life and that He will guide you, in His time, to the peace and joy that will glorify Him most.

Why Does God Allow Pain?

We recognize that the struggle you're facing right now is hard for you. We also recognize that you may end up continuing to struggle with your pain and trials for years. We really do know that pain and sorrow, fears and disappointments are part of what it means to live here in the "not yet." That's where we're living too. Although we fully believe that God can, and indeed may, completely deliver you from your emotional pain, we also know that sometimes it serves His purposes for you to continue experiencing struggles. Why does God seemingly change some people "overnight" while He calls others to faithfully toil on month after month, or year after year? We don't know the answer to that question - it's been hidden in God's secret counsels. What we do know, however, is that He's given us His Word, and instead of trying to figure out what He's doing in every individual's life and why, we need to pursue what we do know of His plan for us (Deuteronomy 29.29).

Although God doesn't usually reveal to us exactly what He's doing in our lives, He has let us know, in Scripture, some general purposes for allowing suffering. In the rest of this chapter, we're going to try to discern some of God's reasons for our pain. It's important that we do this because we have to view our suffering the way He does. Failure to understand and "get on board" with God's purposes in our lives will result in continued difficulties, not the least of which are confusion and doubt.

Here's the reality: *God doesn't view our pain the same way we do.* We think about pain from the very minuscule yet exceedingly important perspective of our own limited experience. We think that we shouldn't have to suffer, that all suffering is bad, that a pain-free life is God's plan for everyone. Because we subconsciously hold to such beliefs, when suffering comes to us, especially in the form of painful emotions, we respond by trying to circumvent or escape the suffering in any way possible as quickly as possible. Please don't misunderstand - we're not saying that you shouldn't respond to your painful emotions. *What we're saying is that sometimes God's good purposes in our difficulties are viewed by us as something to flee from instead of something to learn from.* In fact, sometimes the very way that He answers our prayers for growth is in the form of our greatest trials. This is how He, in His wisdom and love, has fixed the world and our lives to run, and we need to trust that the One Who created us and knows us intimately knows best how to change us and fill us with His endless joy.

You Deserve Happiness

Recently, on a "home makeover" show, we heard an interesting comment. When explaining how the project team had built a large and elaborate entertainment room for a family, one of the team members said, in essence, "We've built this great room for you guys because you really deserve it!" Although it is good for us to help those who have fallen on hard times, there is nothing in Scripture that supports the idea that anyone "deserves" an elaborate entertainment room with all the most modern gadgets. Let's face it: The advertising executives on Madison Avenue's have sold us a bill of goods, and we frequently allow Madison Avenue's messages to shape our beliefs without giving those messages much scrutiny. Do we believe we "deserve" a pain-free life filled with all the most current toys? Is that what the Bible tells us to expect? We know the answer to that question, don't we? The Bible doesn't tell us to expect pain-free lives. Rather, it tells us to expect suffering:

> *To you it has been granted for Christ's sake, not only to believe in Him, but also to suffer for His sake* (Philippians 1:29).
> *Even if I am being poured out as a drink offering upon the sacrifice and service of your faith, I rejoice and share my joy with you all* (Philippians 2:17).
> *Consider it all joy, my brethren, when you encounter various trials* (James 1:2).

> *Blessed is a man who persevere under trial; for once he has been approved, he will receive the crown of life, which the Lord has promised to those who love Him.* (James 1:12).
>
> *For to this you were called, because Christ also suffered for us, leaving us an example, that you should follow His steps* (1 Peter 2:21).
>
> *But even if you should suffer for righteousness' sake, you are blessed* (1 Peter 3:14).

The thought that pain-free living should be ours blinds us to the wonderful blessings that come to us hand in hand with afflictions. There is much good that God bestows on us through our trials, and it's important that we not seek to short-circuit His loving plan for us. Instead of focusing on whatever picture you might have of what a blessed life "ought" to look like, why not dedicate yourself to cultivating a more God-centered and realistic view of life? Remember, God will never withhold from you something that you need, nor will he take from you something that you can't serve Him without.

So let's begin now to examine why God allows trials, pain, sin, and trouble. You'll come to learn that God allows (and even uses) suffering for His own glory. You'll also discover that God allows us to experience troublesome feelings so that we'll be driven to Him and to His Son. And you'll see that God allows us to suffer so that we will love Him more fully and appreciate more fully the sacrifices Jesus Christ made on our behalf (points that we will examine in the next chapter).

God Allows Emotional Suffering

For His Own Glory

When pondering the meaning of life, the Puritans in the 1600's asked the question, "What is the chief end of humanity?" In asking this, they were really saying, "What is this all about? What is the goal? What should Christians be focused on?" The way they chose to answer that question is quite enlightening. They said, "The chief end of man is to glorify God and enjoy Him forever."

That's probably not the answer you would get if you interviewed most people today. The Puritans lived in an era full of suffering (including persecution against them), and they believed that everything, including suffering, happened for one purpose only: *God's own glory* (and in His glory, our enjoyment). The Bible bears this out in many places, including Romans 11.36: "For from Him and through Him and to Him are all things. To Him be the glory forever. Amen."

Think about those words. Everything is about Him! Just as the slogan goes, "It's Not About Me." That little saying really does get to the heart of what both Paul and the Puritans said. *Everything is from Him and through Him and to Him and for His own glory!* We know that *glory* is one of those words Christians have overused, and thus it has become somewhat meaningless. But when the Bible talks about God's glory, it has two rich layers of meaning. The first layer is the "praiseworthiness of the Creator; layer two is the praise which this draw from His creatures." Why do we experience trouble and suffering here? So that we will see how great and praiseworthy God is, and so that upon seeing this greatness, we will give Him the praise He deserves.

Now we come to a very difficult question: How does your suffering bring glory to God? In fact, it might seem to you that your suffering is the last thing He should choose to use to glorify Himself. Wouldn't God be more exalted and praised if our lives were free of suffering? Although this seems reasonable, this logic is flawed. It is flawed because the chorus that exalts God when our lives are pain-free is a faint shadow when compared to the deep, resonating hymn of faith that is distilled from the crush soul of a Job who sings, "As for me, I know that my Redeemer lives, and at the last He will take His stand on the earth. Even after my skin is destroyed, yet from my flesh I shall see God" (Job 19:25-26).

What we know of God's ability to sustain, guide, and comfort us if we had never felt the crushing of life's dearest pleasures or trod the gloomy path

That led through the valley of the shadow of death? Even the beloved apostle Paul knew of this truth when he wrote:

> I am convinced that neither death, nor life, nor angels, nor principalities, nor things present, nor things to come, nor powers, nor height, nor depth, nor any other created thing, will be able to separate us from the love God, which is in Christ Jesus our Lord. (Romans 8:38-39)

Paul savored the magnitude of God's love for him in Christ in the midst of intense personal suffering. In the same way, our suffering and trouble teaches us about God's great power, endless compassion, and sustaining grace in ways that we would never learn nor treasure otherwise.

The Witness of Others Who have Suffered

Aside from the testimonies of Job, David, Paul and the Puritans, consider the suffering of more modern-day saints such as Joni Eareckson Tada and Corrie ten Boom. Joni suffered a neck injury as a young woman and has since spent her life in a wheelchair, paralyzed from the neck down. Her testimony to Christ's sustaining power and wonderful grace has encouraged many people, particularly those with physical handicaps.

Corrie ten Boom grew up in Holland during World War II. Because her family provided a safe hiding place for Jews fleeing from the Nazis, they were eventually arrested and confined to concentration camps. Her story of faith in the midst of intense personal suffering serves as an inspiration to many people today. When we think of these women's woes in light of the faithful praise and worship that exudes from their hearts, we begin to get a clearer perspective of how much greater God is than anything this warmth try to sell on - even the thought of a pain-free life.

The Lord will become sweeter and more beautiful to you as He uses your troubles to strip away the scales that blind your eyes from beholding His true beauty. He's teaching you that temporal happiness is nothing in comparison to the glory that is yet to be known by us. God allows emotional suffering to continue in this world because it glorifies Him to do so.

God Uses Suffering to Bring Us Near

C. S. Lewis wrote that God whispers to us in our pleasures and shouts to us in our pain. Although most of us want pain-free lives, God has obviously decreed that pain-free living isn't best for us. It is true that God has placed within us all the desire for the happiness that pain-free living seems to promise. Our problem is not with our desire for the happiness of ourselves and others. The problem that we have is that we think that true happiness comes from someone or something other than God. God's goal is that we experience true, endless happiness, and He knows where that happiness and joy come from. True happiness and joy come as we are changed to become more and more like Christ. God's goal in our suffering is to make us more like His Son, as Romans 8:28-29 teaches:

> We know that God causes all things to work together for good to those who love God, to those who are called according to His purpose. For those whom He foreknew, He also predestined *to become conformed to the image of His Son* (emphasis added).

God wants us to be like His Son so that we'll find the real joy He's lovingly planned for us. It's easy for us to think that we would be completely whole and satisfied with life in the here and now if everything would just line up with our wishes. But it's in the very withholding of our desires (even those that seem good in themselves!) that the Lord lovingly teaches us the deeper delights found in Himself.

In addition to this compassionate sharing of Himself with us, God also uses our suffering to woo us closer to His heart. Frequently we don't recognize our great need for Christ or our great need to rely on God until we're faced with a difficult circumstance or uncomfortable emotion. Our unhappy feelings tell us that there's something wrong with life as it is here, and that's just what God wants us to learn. God is speaking loudly to us in our pain. Do you hear what He's saying?

The writer of Psalm 119 echoed these thoughts in several verses. Let's consider some of them:

> *It is good for me that I was afflicted, that I may learn Your statutes* (Psalm 119.71). What is God teaching you through your affliction? What are you learning about His Word? Can you see any way in which your trouble has been good for you?
> *Before I was afflicted I went astray, but now I keep Your Word* (Psalm 119.67). Has the affliction you've gone through with your emotions helped you to become more obedient? God's purpose in your suffering is that you learn to obey Him, no matter how you feel. He's also using your troubles to tether you closely to Him so that you won't go astray. Have you looked at your pain in this way? Is God using your suffering to keep you close to Himself?

I know, O Lord, that Your judgments are righteous, and that in faithfulness You have afflicted me (Psalm 119.75). Do you know, in your heart of hearts, that God's judgments and laws are completely and always right? More pointedly, do you believe that His dealings with you are honorable and upright? Do you believe that His plan your life is beyond reproach? Has He not only been faithful to stay with you in your affliction but also in afflicting you so that you would know and love Him more deeply?

I am exceedingly afflicted; revive me, O Lord, according to Your Word (Psalm 119:107). The psalmist experienced exceeding afflictions, but he looked to the Lord to revive him through His Word. In the past, you may have tried to find scriptural help to revive you, and that's part of what we'll do together in this book, but what we want to ask you now is this: Is God's Word the source of your strength today? Do you ask Him to illuminate your heart to His Word so that today, and just for today, you'll have the revived heart that you'll need to make it through?

Responding to Your Suffering in Faith & Hope

As we come to the end of this brief discussion on suffering and God's uses of it, let's look at two more passages of Scripture. First, let's listen to these words from Paul:

In this house we groan, longing to be clothed with our dwelling from heaven . . . For indeed while we are in this tent [he's referring to his physical body], we groan [he's referring to his inner person], being burdened... Therefore, being always of good courage... *for we walk by faith, not by sight...* we also have as our ambition, to be pleasing to Him. (2 Corinthians 5:2, 4, 6-7, 9, emphasis added)

Paul was burdened and felt crushed in his inner person. Have you ever felt burdened and crushed? But even though Paul was suffering so, he didn't allow his feelings to dictate his faith or his actions. Instead, he chose to "walk by faith" and live his life out (even in his suffering) seeking to please God. The psalmist expressed the same determination in Psalm 42:

Why are you cast down, O my soul? And *why* are you disquieted within me? Hope in God, for I shall yet praise Him *for* the help of His countenance. O my God, my soul is cast down within me; Therefore I will remember You... Why are you cast down, O my soul? And why are you disquieted within me? Hope in God; For I shall yet praise Him, The help of my countenance and my God. (verses 5-6, 11)

The psalmist's experience of despair was real, but it wasn't more real than his faith. He believed that God would help him because God was near to him. He determined to remember God, and he believed that one day his countenance would change. He believed that a time would come when he would again praise God and his feelings would be lifted up. Not only did the psalmist force his faith to inform his emotions, but he also let his faith correct the wrong thoughts his feelings were producing. He asked himself, "Why are you in despair? Why have you become disturbed within me?" His faith worked to remind him that what he was experiencing today was not necessarily what he would experience tomorrow. He also remembered that his emotional experiences were not necessarily speaking the truth to him about God and his situation. And so, he placed his hope in God's ability to help him.

As we end time together in this chapter, let us ask you: Do you have hope? Do you believe that the God [W]ho promised He would never leave you nor forsake you is *with you right now*? Do you believe that though you feel afflicted and discouraged, the living God [W]ho loves you with the same love He lavishes on His Son (John 17:23) will strengthen, enlighten, and encourage you?

Even if your honest answer to these questions no, don't despair. God is stronger than your emotions and is able to pull you up our of the miry pit. Trust in Him and remember that you're not alone in this. He's right there with you, and He won't leave.

When we struggle with our emotions, the only sure footing that we can find is in Scripture. Ultimately it really doesn't matter that our friends are encouraging us or that we've convinced ourselves that we are getting better. What really matters is that God is there, understanding, upholding, protecting, and pitying us. So even if you don't feel like doing the study questions that follow,[2] just start with one question and read the Scriptures ... And then move on, as you are able, to the next. We know God will be faithful to meet you.

---

2 The study questions have been omitted from this book. Please refer to page 76 in their book.

The Normalcy of PTSD

This chapter was not on my original list of chapter titles. However, after researching I have concluded that it is necessary and could be very healing to those who live with PTSD.

It is possible that the most intractable prejudice regarding PTSD has been that those who succumb to mental problems due to war or some other trauma are somehow inherently weaker in either body, character or both. Many people still hold to this position despite the fact that after 150 years of study there are still no reliable predictors for who will be affected by traumatic experiences, nor circumstances.[3]

Roy Grinker and John Spiegel observe that psychological deficiencies as a result of combat leave no one immune to the long term effects. "If the stress is severe enough, it strikes an exposed 'Achilles' heel' and if the exposure to it is sufficiently

---

3 Penny Coleman, <u>Flashback. Posttramatic Stress Disorder, Suicide, and the Lessons of War.</u> Beacon Press, Boston, MA, 2006. Pages 19-20.

prolonged, adverse psychological symptoms may develop in anyone."[4]

Therefore, one of the most vital and freeing things that I have learned is that anyone, exposed long enough and deep enough to trauma will in fact, develop PTSD. It is an utterly normal response to life's greatest challenging moments. This was a healing thought for me. It is not due to some inherent character defect or weak genes. It is due to being human.

The fact is that people can often times recover from horror, fear, shock or a combination of moral grievances, even combat stress, if there is a trustworthy support structure in place or if what is "right" has not been violated.[5] When there's no support structure, however, the breakdown seems nearly inevitable. The same stressors, weighing on us alone rather than in tandem, will be far more difficult and can be far more devastating.

Only recently has it become understood that a stress response is intractable, unpredictable in its onset and irreparable. New treatment guidelines accept that given adequate stress, a trauma response is inevitable and universal.

It is normal.

---

4 Roy Grinker and John Spiegel, <u>Men Under Stress</u>, Irvington, New York, NY, 1979. Page 53.

5 Ibid, p. 22.

To further emphasize this point I would like to quote Judith Herman who so appropriately stated the truth this way: "Rape, battery, and other forms of sexual and domestic violence are so common a part of women's lives that they can hardly be described as outside the range of ordinary experience. And in view of the number of people killed in war over the past century, military trauma, too, must be considered a common part of human experience; only the fortunate find it unusual."[6]

Each moment of combat imposes a strain so great that men will break down in direct relation to the intensity and duration of their exposure. For that reason, psychiatric casualties are as inevitable as gunshot and shrapnel wounds in warfare.[7] I would add that this is true throughout life. Many people experience trauma in normal, every day life that is outside a war zone, yet we seem to think that the traumas that come as a result of child abuse, bullying, sexual abuse and so forth could not have the same damaging psychological impact that combat experiences have. This is simply not true.

It is incumbent upon the medical community to lead the way in recognizing the severe and painful results in people's lives so that society can follow suit in validating and not condemning those who suffer irreparable harm from life's darkest experiences. Perhaps most important is the fact that those who have

---

6 Judith Herman, <u>Trauma and Recovery</u>, Basic Books Publisher: New York, NY, 1997, p 33.

7 John Appel and Gilbert Beebe, <u>Preventive Psychiatry: An Epidemiological Approach</u>, p 1470.

perpetrated the abuses and imposed the trauma would take responsibility for the damage that they have left behind in people's lives and finally cease these abominable courses of action.

It still stuns me the degree to which people will minimize the horror and the damage that their own bad characters, lack of coping skills, etc. inflict upon others. They leave behind damaged and shaken people who take days, weeks or even years to get over the violence of the experience and the perpetrators of the violence do not show remorse nor appologize, seek forgiveness or share a moment that would heal. Parents, for example, who deny the pain that their children feel, and the damage that they have done to their offspring, cannot reasonably expect to have a child who will be whole. Neither can society. The validation of someone's pain is integral to his or her healing. Since so many who have caused these traumatic moments will not accept responsibility for their actions, it is significant to note that society can promote healing by acknowledging a person's suffering. This helps them move on. We need "permission" to feel the pain. Validation is vital.

I have tried to explain the changes trauma causes in terms such as "it takes up a residency inside of you, it becomes a part of you and you cannot just shake it off or walk away." It seems to pick a place to "live" and we cannot, as sufferers, figure out where exactly that is and hence cannot uproot it is there all the same, though, eating away at our peace and plaguing us with its habitual intrusion into daily life.

Now researchers are saying it differently. Dr. Jonathan Shay has concluded that there is actually a change in the brain chemistry of individuals due to the traumatic experience. He states that this turns "what was a relatively fluid propensity into a hard-wired reality."[8]

Given what I have learned about emotional release from Dr. Bradley Nelson and *The Emotion Code,* I have to agree with his conclusion. Personally, it makes perfect sense and articulates that which I had not found the words to say.

Dr. Nelson explains these trapped emotions as balls of energy that pick specific places within our bodies to reside and negatively affect our health and our lives. They exert some level of control over our decisions and responses in life, and they can sabotage us without us even being aware of it. Now there's a way to release them and be free of them. Using the emotion code we can release these toxicities and begin to live fuller, happier lives.[9]

Ahh! Validation is indeed healing. Thank you, gentlemen, for helping me put into words that which I have struggled for so long to say. My deepest gratitude to you both.

---

8 Jonathan Shay, <u>About Medications for Combat PTSD</u>, Oct. 1, 1995, www.dr-bob.org/tips/ptsd.html.

9 Please see the chapter on the Emotion Code for further details.

The Stresses of PTSD

The stress factors that PTSD sufferers and those around them must face are far too innumerable to list, yet they are very real in their sometimes overwhelming impact in people's lives.

This chapter has an unusual focus. It is intended for the victims who suffer directly with the illness and its challenges as well as those that interact with the victims impacted with PTSD. I hope to encourage both and to illuminate the minds of those who are in neither category so that compassion and encouragement would flow out to people who find themselves confronted with these issues.

All of us deal with the typical stressors in life such as family, job, illness, physical problems, emotional roller coasters, co-workers, finances, unemployment, homelessness, drug addiction, alcoholism and myriads of other things. But add to this the rantings and ravings of people who are in rage one moment in a flashback and then weeping and broken the next, begging for forgiveness for being so violent and angry. The exhaustion can cause one to turn to drugs and alcohol for relief, for sleep, for blessed unconsciousness. However, relief does not seem to come, even by that means.

Whether you are the one raging or the one being raged at, the one using the drugs and alcohol or the one watching someone selfdestruct with these things, whether you are the one wanting only to die or the one trying to muster up the emotion to care enough anymore if the person dies or not... Whichever side you find yourself on, you are under enormous stress. And what if the person actually succeeds at suicide? How do you then deal with it all when you are already emotionally and physically drained?

These issues are very real for those dealing with PTSD and those who are involved in their lives. PTSD causes confusion and pain beyond the every day sorrows of life. It can be overwhelming and discouraging, to say the least. The feelings of failure for people on both sides of the problem are very real. Guilt from being so overcome by PTSD that just functioning daily is difficult, if not impossible, and guilt from being unable to hold down a job and thereby being a burden to friends and family.

The challenges are real because the pain is real. And the pain impacts the lives of people on all sides of someone with PTSD. While exasperation may be a tempting emotion to indulge in when it is not you who suffers I want to say that only compassion is right. Weep with those who weep, mourn with those who mourn. If your friend or family member is struggling to deal with the after-effects of trauma and overwhelmed by it, then condemning them or yelling at them will not solve or resolve anything. You may feel better for the moment but long term it will only serve to alienate you from a victim that needs you and will close off with respect to you because s/he cannot trust you with the pain and vulnerability that accompany the suffering.

Fear of you and your negative responses will nearly guarantee withdrawal. The victim is in need of having others close, yet s/he simultaneously drives people away out of fear and shame and a host of other possible emotions.

Never doubt that one who suffers with PTSD wants to be rid of it and live a normal life again, whatever *normal* would be! (Some of us cannot even imagine or recall what that would be like!) We not only desire to be rid of it, but we also want to protect others from the consequences and impact of PTSD even though we cannot protect ourselves.

It is never going to be enough to simply tell someone that s/he lacks faith and that we have a big God, or to think positive despite that these violent and intrusive thoughts are unrelenting in their attacks. Those types of statements are so short-sighted and devoid of understanding in the realities of what happens to someone who experiences life-changing trauma. It is as though a switch were thrown inside the body and the mind and the trauma takes up residence inside of the person and makes a home there. It is unwanted and unwelcome, yet it stays as a permanent house guest all the same, taking over more of life, repeatedly, consuming our time, thoughts, energies and emotions. It wears us down and wears us out.

So how do we deal with it? What do we do when we are afraid to go home because we may have violent spells that just seem to have to run their course and come out? Or we are afraid because someone else is going to be experiencing a flashback and we are unable to get any rest because of his or her nightmares every night? Will the person be intoxicated? Passed out? Dead? What do we do with these stresses? Or will it be us ourselves that gets drunk and attempts - or succeeds at - suicide? Do we dare be alone? Is there even a choice? Home can feel like it is our only safe place, and at the same time it can feel like a prison cell because we must battle our demons there entirely alone.

One of the key elements to focus on is prayer. It is not simply praying to "our higher power" as if it does not matter to what or to whom we direct our desperate pleas for help. Rather, the object of our faith must be endowed with the power to be victorious over these life-crushing issues. The only God I know of Who is able to give us the strength to persevere is Christ Jesus, my Lord. No other person has been victorious over the powers of sin and death and Hell and is now seated in victory and authority over them. There is no other source for victorious overcoming power than Christ.

There is also the fact of the possibility of demonic involvement in the lives of people who have PTSD. For example, the North Vietnamese used spiritual combat against Americans during the Viet Nam war. This may sound insignificant but it is hardly trivial. It was a time of fomented all-out rebellion in the United States that could not help but find its way into the military ranks. Rebellion is likened in Scripture to witchcraft because it gives place to the devil, as does letting the sun go down on your anger (1 Samuel 24:11; Ephesians 4:26,27).

The North Vietnamese used voodoo and black magic to attack Americans spiritually. There is good reason to believe that many

Americans, unsaved and hence unprotected spiritually, and in a state of rebellion that made them even more susceptible to demonic attacks or possession, became demonically possessed and have never realized this fact. It is possible that the thought has never even crossed their minds. Not only do they need personally to take the step of faith to believe in Christ and then, with the very presence of God now resident within them to help them, have themselves prayed over and delivered from the demonic strongholds in their lives. This would significantly alter their mental and emotional states for the better.[10]

It is understood in Christian counseling circles that unless there is an absolute physical cause of someone's mental illness i.e., traumatic brain injury, genetics, Alzheimer's disease, etc., then the mental illness is a spiritual problem. Receiving the indwelling of the Spirit of God does much to straighten out our thinking, and demonic deliverance, if it applies, takes this even further. In fact, if someone is having demonic problems, there will be no victory over those issues until the victory is first realized spiritually over the powers of darkness that are the first cause.

Salvation does not automatically deliver us from demons or demonic strongholds; they do not just up and vacate because the

---

10 While doing seminary research I had come across information that stated the normalcy of performing deliverance ministries for people who were saved. Demonic possession in the early church was so extremely common that they usually prayed over each convert to break any demonic strongholds the person had in his or her life. We almost never do this for people any more and yet Satan is at least as active today, the End Times, as he ever was.

Lord saves us. But unless somebody becomes genuinely saved, no attempt at deliverance should be made! The demon(s) would leave, yes, but would return with seven more friends and reoccupy, making the state of the person worse after than before. Unless the indwelling presence of Christ and the Spirit of God are there the person will be able to be reoccupied again very easily (Matthew 12:29, 43-45; Mark 3:25-27; Luke 8:1,2; 11:19-26).

Matthew 8:28-34 relates the following story:

> "When He had come to the other side, to the country of the Gergesenes, there met Him two demon-possessed men, coming out of the tombs, exceedingly fierce, so that no one could pass that way. And suddenly they cried out, saying, 'What have we to do with You, Jesus, You Son of God? Have You come here to torment us before the time?' Now a good way off from them there was a herd of many swine feeding. So the demons begged Him, saying, 'If You cast us out, permit us to go away into the herd of swine.' And He said to them, 'Go.' So when they had come out, they went into the herd of swine. And suddenly the whole herd of swine ran violently down the steep place into the sea, and perished in the water. Then those who kept them fled; and they went away into the city and told everything, including what had happened to the demon-possessed men. And behold, the whole city came out to meet Jesus. And when they saw Him, they begged Him to depart from their region."

Luke 8:26-39 tells the same story with new details that lend insight in this discussion:

"Then they sailed to the country of the Gadarenes, which is opposite Galilee. And when He stepped out on the land, there met Him a certain man from the city who had demons for a long time. And he wore no clothes, nor did he live in a house but in the tombs. When he saw Jesus, he cried out, fell down before Him, and with a loud voice said, 'What have I to do with You, Jesus, Son of the Most High God? I beg You, do not torment me!' For He had commanded the unclean spirit to come out of the man. For it had often seized him, and he was kept under guard, bound with chains and shackles; and he broke the bonds and was driven by the demon into the wilderness. Jesus asked him, saying, 'What is your name?' And he said, 'Legion,' because many demons had entered him. And they begged Him that He would not command them to go out into the abyss. Now a herd of many swine was feeding there on the mountain. So they begged Him that He would permit them to enter them. And He permitted them. Then the demons went out of the man and entered the swine, and the herd ran violently down the steep place into the lake and drowned. When those who fed them saw what had happened, they fled and told it in the city and in the country. Then they went out to see what had happened, and came to Jesus, and found the man from whom the demons had departed, sitting at the feet of Jesus, clothed and in his right mind. And they were afraid. They also who had seen it told them by what means he who had been demon-possessed was healed. Then the whole multitude of the surrounding region of the Gadarenes asked Him to depart from them, for they were seized with great fear. And He got into the boat and returned. Now the man from whom the demons had departed begged Him that he might be with Him. But Jesus sent him away, saying, 'Return to your own house, and tell what great things God has done for you.' And he went his way and proclaimed throughout the whole city what great things Jesus had done for him."

The most significant item to note for this discussion is that once the demons were gone the man was "sitting at the feet of Jesus, clothed and in his right mind." When demons possess someone, they greatly impact the person's thinking in the worst possible ways. It is very possible that numbers of prisoners who are infamous for violent crimes were demonically possessed and under demonic control, and remain so today. While it is not absolutely necessary, in light of the depravity of man and the innate ability that we possess to sin greatly, but it could very possibly be the case.

I bring this up under the heading of stressors because dealing with spiritual warfare is one of the single greatest stressors that I have ever experienced. It exacerbates any problem, any situation, and makes it a living Hell that simply cannot be put into words. Life is hard enough as it is, but add to it a demonic attack and it goes right over the top!

Furthermore, the mark of Satan and his demonic hosts is death. And suicide is a continual threat or temptation that especially those with PTSD suffer with. It is entirely possible that demons are involved in destructive threats of suicidal tendencies that will not abate until battle is done in the heavenlies for that person's soul. Only those who are genuinely saved will be able to do this battle effectively. Demonic forces are well aware of who is genuinely saved, and possessing Holy Spirit power and

44

authority to command them, and those not indwelt by the Spirit of God! They will retaliate without hesitation against the unsaved of attempts to control them are made! Acts 19:13-17 tells us of just what happens when those who do not know Christ as their Savior attempt to battle demonic forces in their own power rather than in the power of God:

> "Then some of the itinerant Jewish exorcists took it upon themselves to call the name of the Lord Jesus over those who had evil spirits, saying, 'We exorcise you by the Jesus whom Paul preaches.' Also there were seven sons of Sceva, a Jewish chief priest, who did so. And the evil spirit answered and said, 'Jesus I know, and Paul I know; but who are you?' Then the man in whom the evil spirit was leaped on them, overpowered them, and prevailed against them, so that they fled out of that house naked and wounded. This became known both to all Jews and Greeks dwelling in Ephesus; and fear fell on them all, and the name of the Lord Jesus was magnified."

There is no conceivable way that anyone will ever be able to beat God, and there is no way that mere mortals can prevail against demonic forces in their own flesh. The only power sufficient for battling such forces is Christ, to Whom all demons are subject. *Salvation is absolutely critical to this fight.*

Please pray for those burdened with PTSD. Because life is so much more chaotic or stressful with PTSD, it becomes more clear how vital intercessory prayer really is. As a coping strategy, it is the best one that I know of. A day hemmed in prayer usually does not see me unravel as it unfolds.

45

The Chronic Pain & Suffering of PTSD

What we go through

One of the greatest aspects of suffering with PTSD is that it is a painful experience which is usually not visible to the naked eye. People think that you look normal and that the "pain" cannot really be that bad (indeed, what pain?). Yet the psychological, emotional and physical drain continues day and night, unrelentingly, leaving the sufferer to feel ever more isolated and alone. There is a cycle of withdrawal that continues inwardly in the victims of PTSD. We try to protect others from our pain, and ourselves from the rejection and lack of understanding we experience when they learn of our suffering. It becomes an ever-increasing battle. The need and desire for deep, intimate relationships grows while the circle of friends who fill those needs shrinks. The pain that it causes makes us withdraw even more into ourselves for further protection.

There is an experiential lack of understanding that people without PTSD have. It can result in a lack of compassion or empathy and cause rifts between people that simply cannot be overcome by conversation. Kindness and compassion are key elements in relationship with those who have PTSD when you cannot comprehend the daily, moment-by-moment anguish of such suffering. But what is typically found in society is that people make comments that are scathing, even hateful, impatient and angry. "Why don't you just get over it?!" or "You're still thinking about that?!" and "What is your problem?! Move on!" and so forth. Their anger, disgust, frustration and impatience are vented outwardly at the victim further isolating the person and causing even greater pain. This lack of understanding, the rejection, and the criticism produces even greater withdrawal. These blasting remarks are the last thing that anyone suffering needs to hear.

The self-righteous pride is devastating to the one sliced into little pieces by the tongue of the uncompassionate fool.

If trauma were so easily side-stepped PTSD would not exist, for everyone who has it would have gotten over it! Yet the assaults of people who have no clue what it is to suffer this way continue unabated. They may deny the sufferer's right to feel pain at all, the truth of what s/he suffered (this is especially true if that person is implicated in the horror that left somebody with PTSD), or they fail to acknowledge the victim's difficulty digesting the events and the emotional impact on the other person.

These social failures can often have two negative consequences. First, it is exhausting to those who are trying to support victims of PTSD. And secondly, it can sometimes exacerbate people's desires to commit suicide. Depression becomes suffocating and failure in every aspect of one's life seems to set in with a force that cannot be met in the weakness that the bearer has. The body is wracked with exhaustion from the lack of sleep and the adrenalated flashbacks. Drugs are used to try to calm the mind. Medication is used that produces a personality that had not existed and usually is not pleasant or easy to deal with. The emotions are up and down, the mind cannot think straight from the drugs, exhaustion, emotional turmoil and so forth. It is impossible to fully explain the full impact of society's failures to comprehend, or even try to comprehend, what those with PTSD are going through.

The psychological, emotional, spiritual and physical sufferings of PTSD are usually only evident to those close to the sufferers or when drug addiction and alcohol consumption take over their lives. As their self-loathing increases so does the pain that they may be causing those who love them to experience. Their depression deepens and their social withdrawal appears to be a solution to protect those around them from the destructive forces inside and out, and to protect themselves from the painful responses of others.

There is no doubt that those who endeavor to be in the lives of those with PTSD have a difficult situation to deal with quite frequently. Yet their presence is so important to the one who feels so very alone in his or her suffering. Though the victim may yet commit suicide it is usually not the fault of those who are around them. Untold numbers of family and friends are dealing with the aftermath of suicide, or attempted suicide, and bearing guilt that simply is not theirs to carry. This book is for them, too, just as the pain of PTSD has spread to include them in its web.

Yes, the chronic pain of PTSD is very much an inward reality and a social struggle of monumental proportions that ultimately seems somehow to include the whole of society. Complicate that with the fact that many people do not even know that they have some measure of PTSD and do not know what to do with the challenges that are faced whilst trying to be normal, all the while wondering, "What is wrong with me?" Without a proper diagnosis it is impossible to operate in light of what is true. If someone has PTSD s/he will struggle to be a part of normal society, all the while feeling isolated and cut off inside; the inward reality of being an outsider can be overwhelming and lead to greater depression and isolation, more withdrawal, more drugs and alcohol, etc.

How we heal Biblically

So What Do I Do With My Pain?

Our response in the midst of our pain to our pain will ultimately determine our success at overcoming it. So answering this question is very important. I have also included a chapter specifically about questions of suffering per se.

Suffering in this world is the result of the presence of sin. Most often we suffer because either we sinned or someone sinned against us. Yet, generally speaking, even bad weather and accidents happen because of the presence of sin in the world, regardless of moral culpability. It is important to note that this life will always have suffering in it even for those who are living right; anyone can have a car accident and everyone experiencess death sooner or later.

The Bible speaks of suffering as a standard experience of every Christian, indeed, every person. It is a given. But the Bible also speaks of the fact that God is up to doing something in His children's lives - transforming and perfecting us into the image of His dear Son, Christ (Romans 5:1-5, 8:28-29; James 1:2-8; 1 Peter 1:3-9). Suffering is an essential factor in our growth and development throughout life, and there is surely no exception in the life of a Christian! Remember that God has a purpose for our greater good. Have faith in His divine character. This can serve to strengthen and encourage us in our struggles as we seek to persevere, to carry on in spite of our struggles. Yet so often what we do is allow our experiences to shape our theology of suffering rather than having our theology shape our interpretation and responses to our sufferings. Admittedly it is a mental struggle due to the shear volume of suffering and the overwhelming experience it is to be habitually assaulted by it. Additionally, our lives have been inundated with errant worldviews, views sadly lacking in any sound theological content.

Our ultimate goal in suffering should be to glorify God and secondly our transformation into the likeness of the Savior. These goals necessitate that God would redeem our suffering so that it would lend meaning and purpose to our lives and the lives of others. Maybe it could even become healing to others because of the mercy and compassion that we can extend to them because of what we have experienced ourselves. It could even become a ministry to others who are hurting in the same manner that we are hurting.

And the apostle Paul says in Romans 8:17 that our suffering confirms our identity with Christ; it does not undermine our identity though it may cause us to doubt God in the crucible of suffering. Rather, as Christians we suffer in Christ. My suffering and my response to my suffering are my identity with my Savior in His suffering. Philippians 3:7-14 says that following:

"But what things were gain to me, these I have counted loss for Christ. Yet indeed I also count all things loss for the excellence of the knowledge of Christ Jesus my Lord, for whom I have suffered the loss of all things, and count them as rubbish, that I may gain Christ and be found in Him, not having my own righteousness, which is from the law, but that which is through faith in Christ, the righteousness which is from God by faith; that I may know Him and the power of His resurrection, and the fellowship of His sufferings, being conformed to His death, if by any means I may attain to the resurrection from the dead. Not that I have already attained, or am already perfected but I press on, that I may lay hold of that for which Christ Jesus has also laid hold of me. Brethren, I do not count myself to have apprehended; but one thing I do, forgetting those things which are behind and reaching forward to those things which are ahead, I press toward the goal for the prize of the upward call of God in Christ Jesus."

The only way we really can make our suffering count for the benefit of others is to share it on some level in a gentle, God-honoring manner. It is my hope that I will accomplish that through this book. May it help many heal.

But what about your suffering? It is critical that hope for overcoming suffering be anchored in the character of God and the knowledge that we have a great High Priest, Jesus Christ, Who shares in our sufferings and Who truly knows what it is to suffer. Isaiah 53 foretold of His sufferings and the gospels relate the horror of His crucifixion. Because He was abandoned and forsaken in His suffering, He is able to guarantee us that He will never leave or forsake those who put their faith in Him (1 Peter 1:11; Matthew 28:18-20). Despite the loneliness of our struggle, we do not have to be alone; He will keep us company along the way as we trust in Him and seek Him, as we learn of Him and believe His promises and put our hope in His character and His purposes for us. As we meditate on these things, it will buoy the sinking heart and the failing spirit. My hope is in my eternal God making my living Hell be to the praise and glory of His grace.

If you do not know where to go in the Scriptures to look for comfort like this than please consider the following: Psalms 13, 22, 77, 88; Isaiah 53; First and Second Peter (written to those who are suffering); Hebrews (which tells of Christ as our suffering High Priest Who is touched by our infirmities and cares). Study the sufferings of the apostles Paul and Peter and the suffering of present day believers around the world who are being persecuted for their faith in Christ. Read the stories of martyred saints throughout history. More Christians were martyred for their faith in the last 100 years than in the rest of history combined. It may comfort you to know that you are not alone in your trials, that the fact of trials is not unusual or strange in some way (James 1:2-4; 1 Peter 1:6,7). Realizing the universality of suffering and pain can lift a burden that is all its own. Though many will never understand what it is to suffer with PTSD, there are many who do. This is comforting.

It is not necessary to be defined by our suffering. We can choose to be defined by our identity as believers in Jesus Christ. He can help us to avoid the extremes of self-indulgent thinking or stoicism in our responses to others. We need not be defeated in hopelessness or defend ourselves in self-righteous anger. Yet because God is molding and shaping us through our suffering, it is in fact shaping our interactions and relationships with others. But it need not destroy them - or us.

Look outside of yourself for a way to serve others and invest in them. Choose an eternal focus. If you are confined on account of your condition, can you help someone by being a listening ear? By praying for people constantly? If you realize that your pain dominates your conversations, as it dominates your life, then work on learning to listen to others. Whatever you do, shift your focus to others and get it off of yourself. Invest in somebody's life, mentor a child, or do community service. This will help everyone, but no one more than yourself. Pray for ministry opportunities. Let the spirit of Christ flow through you as you learn to yield your flesh to the control of the Holy Spirit so that the pain and suffering do not control your actions, your words, and your life.

Depression

What we go through

Depression. Just the word evokes sadness and gloom in many people. For others it is or has been a way of life, sometimes for as long as they can even remember.

J. K. Rowling, in the Harry Potter series, dredged up the Dementors from her memories of depression. They suck all of the life out of you, all the joy. You feel like you will never be happy again. They are dark, foreboding, frightening. The experience is overwhelming and engulfing. You are swallowed up whole by the darkness. It's suffocating.

It can be inescapable. Sorrow or sadness beyond description, beyond reckoning. Beyond words. Beyond hope, beyond help.

Depression is the surrounding and engulfing in a darkness unspeakable. It is pain that never relents of its tormentings, its suffocations.

It cuts us off from others, drives us to seek refuge in solitude to comfort ourselves and then leaves us engulfed in the loneliness of it all. It seems to be never-ending. Situations that drive us down do not change. Hope does not come and pain does not relent.

Joy has evaporated and is only a memory, if even that. Life, if it can be called that, fades to mere shades of gray. All color, all semblance of life, much less laughter, has faded to be a mere memory that no longer even brings a smile to the face as the depths swallow us whole. Life, as it is, is no longer worth the living, no longer worth getting up for, bathing for, eating for. Only sleep may offer some measure of comfort if it allows an escape from the suffering... If only you can sleep.

Eventually, when there is no other escape, we may choose drugs, alcohol, or even suicide. There is no hope. Our world is rocked by despair and hopelessness. Yet who can be found to help? Who cares? Some may have a support network, but many of us endure the endless waves of loneliness utterly alone, thereby exacerbating the depression substantially. Left to try to climb out of the bottomless darkness, the bottomless pit... alone. The climb is too great, the sorrow too profound. And without someone who understands, it simply is not worth the effort to try to overcome. It is too monumental of an achievement when there is no energy to simply get up and bathe or make a meal. We cannot find the strength nor the motivation to do anything, much less find the solutions to our bottomless darkness we are flailing through.

Death would be welcome compared to this endless suffering in the utter darkness of suffocating despair and agony. Happiness becomes too distant to even recall any longer.

Some of us have been depressed for as long as we can remember. I have been one of them. Having had PTSD at the age of three and depression being an overwhelming symptom, I have found it to be my constant companion, though never my friend. It has bore me to the ground and beaten the Hell out of me. It has consumed my thoughts and dragged me to death's very door. If only there had been a means I surely would have put myself out of my misery.

If you are at this time suffering from profound depression and are in need of someone to talk to please don't hesitate to contact one of the links below: http//www.suicidehotlines.com/national.html

http://addiction.lovetoknow.com/wiki/Depression_Hotlines
www.bipolartreatmentinfo.com

There are people who simply cannot identify with these words, who do not suffer with depression or even bouts of depression, for all practical purposes. Yet others are consumed. What is it? Why do we suffer depression? What do I do to overcome it? What do I do to help others overcome it? Is there a cure to life-long depression?

Those who have a support network can easily wear those people out; it is a strain to be around people who are depressed. The depressed can suck the joy out of the air around them, out of the lives of those who love them or who desire to help them. It is a trial to reach them, much less pull them up out of the horrible pit, out of the miry clay, and help them gain their footing on solid rock. It will almost always take a professional's involvement or a much wiser person than us to make significant, long-term differences in the lives of these people. Do not hesitate to seek help in trying to assist someone dealing with profound depression, especially with godly counsel; and do not hesitate to call 9-1-1 or get the person to an emergency room.

But where do we start if we are that person who is depressed? What is a God-honoring goal? What is a God-honoring approach in order to reach the goal? Let us begin at the beginning.

The Beginnings of Depression

I must begin with the caveat that not everyone's reasons for being depressed are the same. Yet I believe that there are commonalities and similarities that can be addressed and considered as broad ranging. This will be the starting point for the purposes of discussion here.

The truth of the matter is that life has many sorrowful things that happen. Recently there have been major disasters in the world in the countries of Haiti, Japan, Chile, etc. If you live there yourself, or you personally lost someone there, you may be even more sorrowful than those of us removed from it but who are nevertheless impacted by it emotionally. Death comes to us all eventually, people we love leave us never to return. Disaster or disease strikes our loved ones. Or us. There is difficulty in a fallen world.

To respond to these calamities with depression is considered normal. If someone you love dies, depression and sorrow are just going to be a part of the process of grieving the loss.

Other things die, too. Our pets, our hopes. Our dreams die, whether they were for ourselves or for those we love or have invested in. Our economy has failed, our efforts in combat have largely failed. Our government has failed. Our system has failed. We have failed.

This brings mixed emotions to us all. Depending upon where you put your hope you may find yourself lost in despair and hopelessness, depressed to some degree. Things have not gone as we had hoped nor as we planned. We see no way out. There is no way up, and there is little comfort or help at the bottom.

Those who wish to help us quote off Scriptures, as if simply hearing them will bring pain relief. It doesn't. Rather it feels like they do not understand and have trivialized the magnitude of our suffering. Their words, instead of bringing healing, bring only further pain. Their approach, often devoid of compassion, compounded by their frustrations and lack of expertise to help us exacerbates our suffering and our loneliness, compounding our struggle with the complication that no one understands, and thus, we are even more alone after seeking help than we were beforehand. And so we seek for help no longer and begin to spiral downward at an ever-increasing rate. Where is the bottom? No one can say until we find ourselves there. And no arm seems long enough to reach down to us that far...into the darkness. Even God's arm doesn't seem to reach us there.

People chew us out, they scream at us in their frustration. They rage at us in impatience. They abandon us in their confusion and apparent helplessness. They trivialize our suffering, our pain, our confusion, our reasons for being depressed and hence, they believe they are relieving us of our burden but really only making themselves more comfortable by dismissing our troubles for themselves, yet it is not in the least bit helpful to us. They are groping in the darkness as much as we are, but they do not understand what to do for us, and often times we do not know ourselves. Rather than stay and suffer they abandon us in order to seek refuge out of the range of our torment and pain that they may recover some measure of wind in their lungs to replace the suffocating darkness they feel when they are around us. Or worse, they simply dismiss us with a wave of the hand as pathetic, useless, and hopeless.

And so we leave with their negativity now attached to our depths of sorrow and despair and feel worse, not better. A punishment of sorts for having dared to be vulnerable enough to talk to someone about it. We may very well never venture that effort again. Our wounds, now in full hemorrhage, seem irreparable. They are life-long wounds and cannot be undone. But will they ever be able to heal? . . . Will we ever stop bleeding?

How we heal Biblically

How Did We Get Here?

So what do we do? How do we handle these things? How should *they* handle these things?

Often times we did not get to our spot of depression overnight. It often creeps up on us over time, as things in life begin to collapse, sometimes slowly, and our mounting problems become mounting griefs that threaten to overwhelm us.

Others come to the shocking revelation of the adversities of life overnight and are plunged mercilessly down into the pit of despair. And the reality of it all swallows them up in a moment, as life utterly collapses and folds down on top of them.

Life happens and it is often out of the range of our control. If we could only get a handle on things we would fix it! The powerlessness we feel is a huge part of our despair. We would fix it if there were hope that anything we did would indeed offer us a solution, even if it was not a quick fix, so to speak. When life is beyond our control, and these bad things are just happening to us, it can be overwhelming just how powerless and hopeless we can feel. All we can do sometimes is submit to the weight of the world placed on our shoulders, crushing us down under its massive weight. We quit fighting for ourselves, resigned to utter defeat.

Such was life growing up under abuse that had only grown in its shear magnitude and its ever-widening ripples of impact destroying lives. As the years passed by, the devastation and horror set in as new realities, new information, and an expanded grasp of just how abnormal and criminal the abuse really was. I understand why I gave up on life by the time I was three.[11] Hopelessness and depression have been my constant companions as parents, relatives, friends and society buried me under the burden of their moral failure and threw me away as garbage is tossed out.

These burdens of moral failure, relational failure, toxic cruelty, suffocation, hopelessness and the lack of opportunity to progress in cognitive development as a child normally does left me scarred emotionally, and, physically. But the most important and significant damage was psychological. Thought patterns were set that could only be called negative and defeatist in nature and hence set up a pattern for failure in every area of my

---

11 Using the Emotion Code and clearing revealed to me both the fact of my overwhelming depression having begun by age 2 and having become desperate by age 3. I have never lived, that I can recall, without being swallowed by depression. The emotion code clearings also revealed that I had PTSD in complete form by the age of 3. Truly, life in Hell daily with an ignorant, abusive witch from the deepest, darkest recesses of Hell was more than any child could take. And because no diagnosis was given no help was given and no one intervened in those days with child abuse that was less than near death or was sexual in nature. Help never came.

life. Yet I never understood the root of why I was failing when everyone else was succeeding. Why didn't it ever change? Why couldn't I get a good job? Why didn't anything ever work for me? Why did everyone treat me so poorly? All of it traced back to the negative things I was taught to believe about myself by the time I was three, and really, truly buried me under it all at the age of seven. Without proper help psychologically, spiritually and physically (i.e., removal from the home to a safe place), healing and victory could not possibly come. There are no coping skills for a three year old entombed in the custody of a hateful woman intent on destroying her home with her own hands, just like her mother before her.

The Need to Change our Thinking

The long and short of it all is that we need to examine our thinking. Or we need to have someone who is godly help us examine our thinking. The reality is that we often cannot figure out where our thinking is wrong because we are in so deep or we have been trained for so long to think that it is normal. If we thought we were wrong in our thinking, we wouldn't be thinking that way; we'd change it. We *believe* what we are saying to ourselves and hence we do not really know where change is needed in our thought processes.

"It's hopeless."

"I'm hopeless."

"There is no point in trying."

"There's no way out."

"Everybody would be better off without me."

"I want/need to escape this pain."

"This is never going to end."

"I can't deal with this."

"This is never going to change."

"I've failed."

"I'll never be any good."

"I have no reason to go on."

Whatever we have said to ourselves in the depths of our suffering, we believe it is true. Therefore, the only solution is to relentlessly - and I mean *relentlessly* - pursue God's Truth in Scripture. Yet how do we do this when we are so low we can barely get ourselves to the toilet? And what if we have no clue where to turn in the Bible anyways?

First, I would like to offer to people once again several things. Believe in Christ so that He can enter your journey of suffering personally in order to guide you through. Secondly, seek *godly* counsel. If you do not have that or do not know where to turn to find it, then visit http://www.nanc.org and they will direct you to someone that you can work with. Thirdly, seek out a church that teaches the unadulterated Word of God and get under the preaching and teaching of Scripture, and learn how to study it for yourself.[12] If you get your mind on other things, then your troubles may take a backseat.

---

12 A caveat has to be given here regarding learning how to study the Bible. It is best not to use a typical bookstore as their so-called "Christian section"

Search http://nanc.org/resourcelibrary.aspx for names of reputable publishers. There are others but this is a good place to start. Get affiliated with their "Journal of Biblical Counseling," which can be purchased on DVD and loaded into your system for searching topics or simply reading whatever interests you. It is very handy. The authors that have contributed to the articles often times have also written books that can be searched at Amazon and purchased with a high degree of confidence in their Biblical accuracy.

I would also like to mention that it is important to seek medical care. If the problem is an underlying medical condition, then no amount of Biblical counseling will ever replace good medical care. However, if the proper medical care is given then it is a good possibility that the situation may resolve itself over time as part of the healing process. At bare minimum, it will give you a better fighting chance at overcoming any other reasons for depression.

I have often been told, however, that the predominant reason that people are depressed is because their thinking is wrong. In other words, they are not thinking with truth. That may indeed be true. And if that is "all" that it is, then correcting our thinking would be the solution. While I believe this is an oversimplification of the problem, we nevertheless need to examine our thoughts.

───────────────────────────

is the most anit-christian section in the entire store. Please use reputable websites to find Biblical resources. http://www.ccef.org is a good place to begin. Speak with mentors, pastors, etc.

Thinking on Truth

If the Psalms are examined we find that the writers often times are looking at their physical situation, or their circumstances, and have concluded that life stinks. Yet those that resolve their conflicts, as presented in each psalm, keep coming back to the same thing: God. They recite praises of Him, recite the truth about Him and get His perspective. This, too, is what we need to look at.

For those who groan at the mere thought of trying to corral the mind, lost in fog and confusion, I understand! Yet it is necessary to try and any effort that is made will yield positive results.

Medicine & Depression

There is a line of reasoning in typical medicine these days that heralds a pharmaceutical solution to every malady. One of them is that if you are depressed, then you are in need of medicine, specifically antidepressants. People who advocate this position hold tenaciously to the idea, unproven but roundly touted, that our brains are misfiring, that there are imbalances in the neurotransmitters, etc. They have a host of designer drugs to treat most known psychological imbalances due to physiology. They are inventing new drugs all the time, and then marketing drugs to people for those newly identified ailments.

However, it is just as likely that these drugs will *cause* you depression and sleeplessness, and weight gain and a host of other problems, as it is likely that these drugs will "fix" anything! These well-intentioned scientists believe that we are nothing more than a collection of chemicals that evolved from the muck of the ground and hence all solutions lie in more chemicals being added to the mix. A rebalancing of the chemicals and ...Voila! All is now well!

This misconception, that we are only a collection of chemicals that happened together in the evolutionary process and now survive the environment, has led to a rash of poor counsel and errant treatments, including medical ones. For example, if we have more to our composition than biology, or if we are more than just chemical ooze evolved to be sentient, then we need to address treatments to more than just our chemical make up!

God's Word says that we have immaterial parts, as well as material parts. These immaterial parts, if they are responsible for our depression, will not simply be medicated and wonderfully fixed. We have to address spiritual issues as spiritual issues. And this will take far more than the pharmaceutical industry.

This is surely not to imply that we never have physiological problems that cause depression. Other medications can cause depression. Medical problems for which no diagnosis has been given cause depression. Chronic pain can cause terrible depression as a "switch in the body" seems to be flipped that simply never gets flipped off again.

If you have come down with depression and have no idea what is causing it, in other words, you cannot consciously think of why you are depressed, then please contact your physician immediately and get a full physical. It is possible that you need proper medical treatment before you will find relief.[13]

But when the problems we are facing that cause our depression are very real and identifiable, then we have a heart[14] issue, or an inner person issue, to confront effectively. This is not done by means of medication. Only God can truly cure what ails us at that point. The Spirit is what brings us hope and light. Our distressed minds are able to overcome because of a deliberate alteration to our thought patterns.

Another major contributor to depression is the experience of incessant disappointments. When life fails to live up to our dreams, our hopes or our expectations, we often become discouraged. If we have any theological beliefs, they will be tested. It is in these crucible moments that we may realize that we expected more from God than He has delivered. Perhaps we doubt even

---

13 If you are presently on a regiment of medications please do not cease taking these without consulting your physician. Some medications must be handled with special care and cannot be stopped suddenly without great harm to yourself. Be sure you have expert counsel before stopping any medications.

14 The heart, as used in the Bible, means the mind, the will and the emotions. It is not the cardiac pump in the chest but rather what we think on, what we volitionally choose to do and what we emote. Our emotions are a direct byproduct of what we are thinking on and can, therefore, be directly impacted by changing our thoughts from the wholly negative to the positive. Or, from falsehoods to truth. This is the basis for this chapter's solution, changing our thinking.

76

the existence of God. Maybe it is here that we realize we only worshipped God for what we thought He would give us, or what we thought we could get, and not for Who He is.

Whatever the case, we find ourselves living a life filled with pain. We may very well be disillusioned about something. It is at this point that we need to examine our lives and look for the sources of our depression. It is very possible that we have more than one source of our depression. If we assume that there is only one cause for our depression we may very well miss a big amount of the problem. But if we hit it as a multi-faceted problem, we will be much more likely to find that any number of things contribute positively to solving our emotional difficulties.

Regardless of what the cause or causes of our depression are God can be present in any and all of them and use them to bring us closer to Him. It will require that we work in faith, which can be a difficult task even under favorable circumstances at times, and even more difficult under the fog and darkness of depression. Thinking straight can be a challenge any way that you look at it but thinking straight while depressed can be impossible. Yet God calls us to corral our thoughts and bring them captive to our wills and into obedience to His Word. As difficult as this is, if we succeed at learning this skill through sheer determination of our will and persistent hard work with God's help, we can find spiritual growth in the darkest of times.

It is possible that what God is trying to teach you is His power to sustain you in the midst of suffering. And He may want to show you that through Him there is power to change. If we learn to tap into His power, then we can overcome our depression and bypass any drugs and their ill side effects. We will be transformed in the process.

What's Going on in Your Depression?

All of us are invested in different areas of life. Some have family that they invest in, some more heavily than others. Some invest in their education, their careers, the pursuit of money. What we invest in and the degree to which we are invested in any given area of life at any given moment speaks volumes about us.

When we are disappointed in life, when we become depressed, it is often because we have loss in some area of life that mattered to us greatly. It did not work out the way we hoped or wanted. What we worked so hard for did not materialize. The point is, what is significant to one person is inconsequential to another. Do not be too rash to dismiss these matters when it comes to the causes of your depression. It can be true that we become so accustomed to the numbness that it is our normal. Deadness and emptiness are hallmark defining words for those who suffer with PTSD. We no longer recall what it means to be happy, if we ever knew... Joy, even in the Lord, is elusive or shallow at best. Our emotions have so long been shut down that we no longer know how we shut them down, or when. Turning them back on seems pointless: I would have to feel the pain again and I simply cannot bear it. We hold our breath and try to endure as best we know how. Enduring is all we can do; living is simply out of the question.

While all of this becomes normal to someone who is depressed it is not what God wants us to do. It is not how He wants us to live. He wants us to learn how to handle the pain and work through it.[15] He wants us to address it rather than ignore it. He means for the pain, no matter how unwelcome to us, to prompt us to examine our hearts and grow. If we simply bury it we may never work through it and never move forward past it; it might anchor itself within us so deeply that we cannot uproot it and no longer think about it because it is such an integrated part of us.

When something becomes a large part of your life, your struggles, you may really "set your heart on it," we love it with all of our heart, soul and strength; we love it more than God. Scripture warns us about what we set our hearts upon. Matthew 6:21 states, "Where your treasure is, there will be your heart also." Put simply, if we set our hearts upon something and we loose it or do not get it, we will become depressed. We need to examine this heart response and evaluate whether that thing we treasure is a God-glorifying thing or not. Is it right? We can labor for a soul to be saved and the person die before trusting Christ. This breaks our hearts. This is righteous. But if we labor for a huge promotion or raise and don't get it, and if this causes us major

---

15 Once again, I cannot recommend highly enough using the emotion code to work through these emotional issues that leave us stuck. Emotionally processing all the things that are contributing to your depression is critical in overcoming it. You can also use kinesiology to determine what is causing your depression, all of the separate aspects of it, so you can address all of them individually and be victorious over them. You may very well be surprised at all the threads contributing to your depression.

depression for an extended period of time, then we have an idol to cast down and Christ to raise up in our hearts.

All this is not to say that life's disappointments aren't difficult! We should labor to glorify God and advance in our careers. Hopefully this will put Christ before people and they will see Him in us. But our motivations must constantly be examined and re-examined. We must proceed to investigate the truth of our heart, with the Spirit's help, and the Word of God shining a light on our sin. This is a daily ever-continuing process.

If, on the other hand, you can no longer think of something that you treasure, or can no longer think of something to treasure, seek Christ. The pursuit of the knowledge of God - if persevered after long enough, through all emotional deadness and hopelessness, through all tears and sorrow, through all surrender and grief - will yield a love of His Word and a love for Christ, and all He endured, to make us His own. It may takes months. Sometimes our losses take years to get through. Keep at it. Keep after Him. It will yield the peaceable fruit of righteousness.

We were created to love and worship God and God alone. In spirit and in truth. If - or I should say when - we choose to love something else more, then God then we have set ourselves up to have those idols toppled by a jealous God. He will not share us with lesser gods. He will risk our misunderstanding Who He is and what He is doing to teach us about Himself. To "win" us back to Himself. Some of these methods are quite painful. He means for us to feel pain when we are not right with Him. Being right with God leads us to the fulfillment that only He can give.

But beware! There are traps along the way and the devil is relentless in his pursuit of our destruction, just as much as Christ is faithful in pursuing our transformation into godliness.

I wish someone had told me when I was new to saving faith - or any time sooner would have been great, too! - that the easy life does not exist for most of us. I was raised to believe that if you had tribulation in life it was an unusual thing, not normative. You should get bitter and angry. Explode. Take vengeance upon others for the wrongs that they have done to you. This is simply not a righteous way of thinking, and the response to it is also wrong.

Some are taught - and it is grave error indeed - that once you are saved life should get easier. That, too, is simply wrong. Often times God will leave us in the adversities that have led us to humble ourselves and call upon Him. His reason for doing so is often times to show the world, through us our transformation in the circumstances. This demonstrates salvation and changes lives. It makes way for the sharing of the gospel to those who might never hear the words or have seen the life of faith, the life of change in us.

If your circumstances do not change, then trust that God is at work in you and in those circumstances to bring about something good for you , even though it may not seem like it! When all is lost, He steps in. Not usually in the way that we ask, nor in the way we expect. But He steps in and works all things after the counsel of His own will. He makes things ultimately work out for those who love Him and are called according to His purposes.

I say all of these things because there are those who teach that if you come to faith in Christ and are not blissfully happy, wealthy, healthy and so forth, then you don't have enough faith. This is surely NOT the cure for depression! It is toxic and destructive; it flies in the face of biblical theology. It has caused many people to be grieved beyond words and to spin lower into depression. Wrong counsel is a serious offense to God and should never be taken lightly (James 3:1).

Emotional suffering is a part of life in a fallen world, a world riddled with sin and suffering of all kinds. There are many people in Scripture who suffered with depression. Moses, David, Job, Jeremiah, Paul and most notably, Jesus. Jesus wept at the tomb of Lazarus, his friend. He grieved in the Garden of Gethsemane. He knows our sorrows and He is touched by our infirmities (Hebrews 4:15). He cares for us and hence we can bring our troubles to Him, lay them at His feet and know that all of our deepest pains and sorrows are safe with Him. He will not berate our trust, nor mock our pain. He may rebuke our actions or our errant theology. But a broken and contrite heart He will not refuse (Psalm 34:18; 51:17).

The fact of suffering in the world does not necessitate that God is angry with you or that you have sinned. You may simply be going through difficulties common to all of humanity.

Depression is common to all ethnic groups, to every religious persuasion, including Christians. Men have it, women have it. The young are afflicted, as are the elderly and everyone in between. Neither are there factors that rule someone out as a potential candidate of PTSD. This is not necessarily the discipline of the Lord. It may be a fact of life.

If you are wondering whether you are under discipline or simply suffering in the will of God (and it is the will of God that all will suffer who live godly in Christ, 2 Timothy 3.12) then please do this exercise. Pray, assuming you already know Christ as your Savior, otherwise start with that, and ask God to show you what is going on inside of you. Ask Him to reveal sins that are causing you to loose fellowship with Him, that may cause or contribute to your depression. If, after a faithful period of time, there is no response from God indicating any specific sin or sins, then assume it is a matter of suffering in the will of God and respond righteously.[16] Of the eight processes of growth in the Christian life suffering, or learning endurance, is the fifth. It is simply a fact that we must suffer in this life to mature. How we handle it demonstrates our maturity at that moment. But our response also determines how and if we will grow from the experience and whether we will have to repeat it. Regardless of the source of our suffering a righteous response is always required and it always looks the same: like Christ. If you do not know what it is to suffer righteously then please see my bibliography and pick titles that peek your interest.

God is committed to sanctifying us and making us holy but we have to be patient with the process. Change, especially growth, takes time. He is willing to see us through to completion and

---

16 There is a very helpful book that I was given when I graduated from the seminary. On the point of understanding these issues of growing through adversity, please see *Secrets of the Vine* by Bruce Wilkinson.

we must be willing to do the same. He will indeed help us bear the burdens we have loaded down upon ourselves, including the consequences of our sins. But beware of the fact that the way of the transgressor is hard (Proverbs 13:15). If you attempt to conceal your sin you will not prosper (Proverbs 28:13). Confession of sin and taking responsibility for our wrongs is an integral part to healing our depression. If we are burdened with guilt over our sins it may be one of the underlying causes of our depression. Until it is handled properly our depression will not relent. We will not grow under this burden sin imposes.

No matter how often we commit and then recommit to forsaking sin, God always forgives us when we repent and come to Him for forgiveness. As disgusted as we can become with our sin, our sinfulness, our failures, and our repeated need to seek Him and ask for forgiveness, He always forgives a genuinely repentant heart (1 John 1:9). The lie that God does not want to hear from us again on the same sin that we have come to Him for forgiveness repeatedly in the past is from nothing but the deep recesses of hell. But it can also indicate we have an unbelieving heart. We tend to project our sinfulness upon God and shy away from asking for His forgiveness again because if someone came to us to ask us for forgiveness *yet again* we would surely lose our patience with that person! Wouldn't God do the same with us?! No, He wants to keep the lines of communication open. In Matthew 18:22 He states that forgiveness is to be a habit that we develop and that there is no end to the number of times we are to forgive the sins of others. If someone sincerely repents then we need to forgive that person. This is God's way of doing things for us, too. So do not be shy about going to God again and asking Him to help you try *yet again* to be victorious over the sin that plagues you and keeps you from living a full life in Christ. He is happy to hear from you!

What God May be Up to in Your Depression

In a book that I found helpful there was a passage that the author shared delineating some reasons God allows suffering. PTSD is one form of suffering that encompasses many other forms of suffering. Depression is one of those forms of suffering, and is at the same time a category in and of itself. It seemed appropriate to include it here.

What is God Up To?[17]

"Since we know God is sovereign (He really is in control of everything), there must be a reason He's allowing you to go through this trial. Although we don't know the exact reasons for your suffering, let us remind you of some of the reasons for suffering that were presented in chapter 3 [of her book]:

God uses suffering to draw us to Him. Ask yourself: *Have I been hiding from God, not wanting to experience more pain?* Instead of hiding from Him, why not run to Him as Hezekiah did and cry out for help?

---

17 Elyse Fitzpatrick & Laura Hendrickson, <u>Will Medicine Stop the Pain?</u>, Moody Publishers, pp. 110-111. Italicized portions indicate original authors' italics.

Through suffering we learn to be more grateful for the suffering of God's perfect Son. Ask yourself: *Has the suffering of Jesus meant more or less to me during this time?* If Christ's woes haven't become more precious to you, ask Him to make them so. Remember, "Jesus Christ did not come to take away your pain and suffering, but to share in it."

Suffering is meant, in part, to motivate us to seek to change. Ask yourself: *How willing have I been to look deeply into my heart and ask God to change me? Am I willing to ask God to change me even if that means that my suffering might continue for a while?* Sometimes the thought of having to change (particularly when it seems as if no one else is!) can be daunting. Just remember, your goal isn't to change in response to others. Rather, it's to change in response to the great love of God in Christ (Romans 5.3-5).

Our pain works to reveal our own misconceptions and sins and to lead us to repentance and truth. Ask yourself: *Is it possible that among the reasons I'm suffering is because my thoughts about God are incorrect, or because God is trying to show me ways that I'm sinning by loving something more than I love Him?* God isn't unkind. He doesn't bring suffering or trials into our lives for the fun of it. He's working toward a specific goal: changing us into the likeness of His Son. Sometimes we're unaware of what's happening in our hearts, and the Lord, in His kindness, is seeking to reveal more truth to us through the use of our pain.

Suffering humbles and enables us to comfort others who are suffering. Ask yourself: How has my struggle with this trial made me more aware of my weaknesses? How has this awareness made me more gentle or humble so I can better comfort others? God is interested in using your gifts for the betterment of His Son's bride. In going through this trial, you're being better equipped to serve others in the church who are suffering. It's important for you to remember that your suffering isn't just about you as an individual; it's about you as part of a body that needs your gifts - tempered and refined by fire as they may be (2 Corinthians 1:3-11)."

There's Something You Can Do

If you are able to speak with a good friend about your depression please do so. If you do not have a good friend to turn to, then try finding a NANC counselor or a good church to join. The pastor may be able to help you find someone who will walk with you through your journey and be your friend. I know that this can be unrealistic and many of us must walk utterly alone. Jesus will be your companion. Listen to Him. Everything He says to stir hope in your breast will align perfectly with the written Word, the Bible.

If you are able to find someone to walk with you during your struggle then you will both find it an opportunity to grow together. The first thing you may wish to ask the person to do is to read through this chapter and the chapter on depression in Elyse Fitzpatrick's book, *Will Medicine Stop the Pain?*. Secondly, try praying together on a regular and faithful basis. Get together just to chat, just to be out of the house. If you find it difficult to pray, and that is likely, then ask the other person to do so. Pray when you are alone. Focus attention on things that your friend needs. Turn your focus outward. Study the Scriptures together.

Listen to the perspectives and thoughts that your friend gives you. If you are angered by them, then please don't respond. Give it time and think about it. Don't retaliate. The person just might be right. If you are the person that someone else has turned to, for help then remember that things do not always sink in the first time they are said if someone is in deep depression. Things will have to be repeated, explained in detail with time to think and absorb the truth. They will have to be reminded of what you have said again in the future; our hearts are not always prepared to hear every truth.

Pray back the darkness. Some of it may very well be a demonic attack. If you are a Christian, then learn to recognize demonic attacks; they seem to be more common than we think. You may pray out loud if you wish. Or ask a Christian friend or someone else to pray against the forces of darkness. Read Scripture out loud. This will help you focus on important things and cause the spirits of darkness to flee (they flee at the praise of God and at the hearing of the Word of God). Use the armor of God (Ephesians 6:10-17) and resist the devil so he will flee from you (James 4:7).

If you are under a deep and sustained demonic attack, you will miss that your thoughts do not actually make rational sense any longer. The truth is that only others may be able to detect the foolishness, because your errors will seem reasonable to you! You must use discernment to test them against the Word of God. A question that you may ask yourself is, "What do I know to be true? What do I know to be true of God?" Use sound books on doctrinal theology if you need to study the doctrines. Find someone to disciple you.

God's Word needs to become more real to you than your feelings. This is a difficult journey, to say the least. Feelings can overwhelm us and bury us, suffocate us. Trying to overcome them by thinking differently is a challenge that seems insurmountable! Try anyways. Cry if you need to.

Examine the things that you are responsible for. Are you fulfilling your duties? If you are not, then begin doing so. As you fill your time with more productive things you will see progress gradually, you will begin to feel better. Turn your attention to someone or something outside of yourself. Find someone who needs your help, someone from whom you will gain nothing and help that person. Get involved in volunteer activities that get you involved outside of your home, especially with other people. Try to find meaning and purpose in something outside of yourself and your troubles. Make Christ and serving Him your focus. Try to get involved in something that advances the Kingdom of God. Those are the issues that will matter for eternity. Store up eternal reward for yourself by becoming a deliberate blessing to other people.

Determine concrete steps to get moving. Write them down and post them in several places in your house that you go regularly: the bathroom, on the nightstand, the recliner, etc. Read them and do them.

If you do what is right your countenance will be lifted (Genesis 4:6-7). But do not underestimate that if it took you awhile to get to this point in your struggle then it will take awhile to get back out again. Hang in there.

Cast yourself upon the Lord and He will take you up, up out of the horrible pit, out of the miry clay (Psalm 40:2,3). He knows the way, and His arm can reach to the lowest depths, even to where you are.

Look up and see Jesus.

Suicide

What we go through

My eye wastes away with grief, Yes, my soul & my
body!
For my life is spent with grief, & my years with
sighing;
My strength fails because of my iniquity, & my bones
waste away.
Psalm 31:9b,10

Suicide is the product of a continuous transaction between the person's heart, his symptoms of depression,
the levels and types of stressors in his environment, and
the strategies he uses to cope with his depression and
life circumstances.[18]

If You Are Suicidal

If you or someone you know are considering suicide please seek
help. The U.S.'s suicide prevention lifeline is 1-800-273-TALK
(8255) and the website is http://www.suicidepreventionlifeline.
org . Another is http://www.suicidehotlines.com and the phone
number is 1-800-448-3000. For veterans use http://www.military.
com/veterans-report/suicide-prevention-hotline.html. You may
also call 911 for yourself or others. Or walk into an emergency
room and ask for help.

---

18 Black, Jeffrey, *Suicide. Understanding and Intervention*, p. 13.

Hope

It is now my intent to endeavor to give hope to the hopeless and a reason to live to those who can no longer find one. Because the problems that drive us to suicide are found in this world and overwhelm us, the solutions must be sought for and found in the Bible. Only then will we get the victory over our fleshly desires, especially an overwhelming desire to commit suicide.

It is worthy to note here that worldviews of those who are suicidal are remarkably similar, regardless of his or her spiritual disposition (saved or unsaved). The experience of unbearable pain, interpersonal alienation, and hopelessness is similar. The struggle with unmet felt needs and the belief that there are no solutions to their problems is the same. The difference seems to be that non-Christians have no spiritual light or Biblical truth, and seek help in what we view as worthy of worship, while Christians have light and truth but do not keep their eyes on these things.[19]

While we may believe that our disastrous lives, our unmitigated suffering, is the reason that we wish to commit suicide, I would like to propose that the reason is really a heart issue: what we are thinking is not of eternal value nor eternal perspective. What we need to do is shift our thinking, our focus, from what is here and temporal to what is eternal. The shift in our thinking will help us put things into perspective and give us hope.

I speak from experience and have repeatedly dwelt on thoughts of suicide. PTSD and its attendant suffering is overwhelming

---

19 Black, Jeffrey, *Suicide. Understanding and Intervention*, p. 2.

and its pain endures daily, and sometimes it is very intense. The chronic pains of life, in all its various forms - physical, mental and emotional - are all crushing to the spirit. And a broken spirit is indicative of a broken life, a broken heart. But God does not despise a broken and contrite heart; He will not despise us when we bring it to Him (Ps 51:17).

The suicidal person usually has a sense of psychological pain that is unbearable. The goal may very well involve death indirectly while the primary goal is a reprieve from the pain. Death becomes a means to an end, not the end itself. This is especially true when psychological pain leads to physical pain, such as migraines that rarely subside, or when phantom pain from amputated limbs is still perceived by the mind.

> "As they try to identify the source of the pain, depressed persons may connect it to specific experiences (guilt, shame, loneliness, alienation, abandonment, hopelessness), but will frequently regard it as a pain that overshadows everything. They will also describe their pain in terms of its debilitating effects, both internal (loss of concentration, new fears, inability to make decisions) and external (unemployment, loss of friendships, financial ruin). The extent to which a person sees pain as something ruining his life, especially when he believes that life will be this way forever, is part of the network of beliefs that leads to suicide."[20]

It is still difficult to write about these things. The truths can be very hard to absorb, especially through a mind that is over-

20 Black, Jeffrey, *Suicide. Understanding and Intervention*, p. 14.

whelmed with sorrow or grief, depression or pain. Our thinking is cloudy, everything moves in slow motion. People try to tell you things that just do not sink in; we need to be told the same thing over and over to remember. Memory fails us. We have failed ourselves. We say to ourselves, "This isn't the victorious Christian life that I was promised. . . I feel like such a failure."

"Though the pain of depression can be suffocating, our wills and our moral values are part of every aspect of our lives. Even when there is a biological component to the depression, our interpretations of our experiences - and our responses to them - are rooted in the thoughts and desires of our hearts. What finally determines our experiences and choices is whether we see our lives through the lens of our relationship with Jesus Christ."[21]

If we are suicidal we have shifted our thinking to things here on earth, things that matter more to us than God: the idols of our hearts.[22] Sometimes God allows us these idols, and even permits them in excess, in order to sicken us with respect to them so we will throw them away ourselves (Isaiah 30:22). With other individuals, He may deliberately withhold them until we see that we do not need them, but rather need Him. He wants us to turn to Him and not make something lesser our god.

A common idol of those suffering with PTSD is the desire to be out of pain, whether it is physical or emotional does not

---

21 Black, Jeffrey, *Suicide. Understanding and Intervening,* pp. 3-4.

22 An idol of the heart is anything that we are willing to sin to get, to have or to keep.

98

really matter. We often choose medication or substance abuse to numb, to pass out, to sleep, or to "take a trip." Alcoholism and drug addiction are very common in those who deal with PTSD. Moderation is abandoned for relief. Mixing substances may be more successful in granting a reprieve, in giving us sleep or blessed unconsciousness. Desperation to escape can be the mother of invention and creativity. Our level of experimentation escalates to unsafe degrees and accidental over doses are not unheard of with PTSD.

It is not only our pain that cries out for relief, it is our depression, our hopelessness, helplessness, powerlessness, loneliness, purposelessness (especially an inability to hold down a job, possibly due to substance and/or alcohol abuse and not just PTSD). And there are many other things that contribute to the problem. Usually it is not just one thing that drives someone over the edge but rather a combination of things that, when mixed together, are as toxic to our souls, as lethal as any combination of illicit or prescription drugs. What we seek is relief from our problems, from our thoughts, from our pain, from...life.

So to what - or to whom - do we turn? This is the question.

How we heal Biblically

I would never discourage anyone from talking with loved ones or seeking support groups, or utilizing the VA or other medical services in the handling of depression. These can all be helpful. Seek help here if you need to. However, it is very important to note that none of these things will be as effective as possible without the accompaniment of Christ and having Him walk with you through the process.

In my painful and ongoing struggles with suicidal thoughts I have sought answers and have found some in the seeking. Yet, putting them into practice is easier said than done. When one feels like the pain is unbearable, that it will utterly swallow you up, trying to focus on "things above where Christ is seated at the right hand of the Father" (Colossians 3:1) is difficult. Thinking is already flawed and clouded. How does anyone shift focus from that which threatens to consume us to the spiritual realm, which seems ethereal, so intangible?

When we lose something that causes us to conclude that life is no longer worth living, we have found what we believe life is about. If the loss of a spouse means that you no longer want to live, then your spouse may have been the reason you thought life was worth living in the first place. But God wants to point us towards Himself. Jeremiah 29:13 states, "You will seek Me and find Me when you seek Me with all of your heart." But how often do we do this? God is desiring for us to persevere in suffering. He wants us to rise above it all. It all sounds so very impossible. The only way that we can do so is to put our hope *in Him.*

Many of us keep looking on our lives and our circumstances as the cause of our problems. And, truth be told, they are a huge part. But really they are the litmus test of who we are. They reveal to us who we are at that moment. The accumulation of them and our responses to them make us who we are. If we respond rightly - and who always does that? - then we will be better people for the character shaping that the adversities will perform in us. If we respond wrongly then our trials will also shape us but we will not be better because of them. In Christ we can always be better; there is always a new lesson to learn or one we realize that we have learned and are handling better.

Many people throughout Scripture made many mistakes. Abraham twice lied about his wife. David tried to cover adultery with murder. Solomon destroyed a glorious kingdom with his love of women. Peter denied the Lord Christ during his Savior's worst hours on earth. And there are many more.

My favorite is the Apostle Paul, named Saul before he was gloriously saved by Christ, who is officially recorded as being the chief of sinners. Thus, it stands that the greatest man in the New Testament, apart from Christ Himself, is the worst sinner in history who became a marvelous trophy of God's saving grace and wrote the majority of the New Testament texts! What an incredible God, Who can restore the lives of the worst sinners and make them be to the praise and glory of His grace for all of eternity! Wow!

Whatever we have done, God can restore our lives[23] and give us hope that we do not have apart from Him. So it is my intent here to offer the hope of a changed life, even—or especially when - we are at the lowest point of our lives. Sometimes we have to be in the bottom of the slippery pit to look up and be humbled enough to ask for help (Psalm 40:2).

Often times our depression is complicated by guilt over sins that we have committed. The only solution that I know of is coming to God with a repentant heart and asking Him for forgiveness (the releasing of our sin debt against Him) by faith in Christ or by renewing our fellowship with Him if we are already saved.[24] Yet, if we do not receive this forgiveness by faith and believe that our sin is really gone then we will still be trapped in our guilt and shame. Receiving forgiveness can set us free from the depression that plagues us as a result of these toxic emotions. Our outlook can be transformed when our focus shifts from self-absorbed misery to freedom in the new-found mercies of God. Simply singing hymns or rehearsing Scripture can help greatly.

One of the biggest struggles that I have had to deal with is that of failed dreams. Hopelessness and despair can set in. Meaninglessness. Loss of significance. Whatever we organize our lives around, when it is taken from us we are left feeling

---

23 The restoration of lives broken by sin and life's mistakes is precisely why Christ came to earth. He died on the cross in our place so that we could have our lives redeemed, forgiven and transformed by His saving grace.

24 David says in Psalm 32.5, "I will confess my transgressions to the Lord - and You forgave the guilt of my sin."

empty and despairing. Often times, as was my case, we don't even realize how important those dreams are to our lives until their failure to materialize plows into us like a truck; we didn't know that we organized our hope for the future around something so fleeting.

Our dreams can reveal to us where we found our meaning for living. When what we live for dies, a part of us dies also. Life becomes empty. There can be so much pain that suicide seems like the only alternative, or surely the most appealing one. After all, our body, which feels like a hollowed-out shell, is still living. The rest of our being has died a painful and cruel death. There is no hope left. I had built my life around the hope that my dream would be realized. As unaware of this as I had been, it was clearly futile. And idolatrous.

In those darkest moments, trying to look up and see the goodness of God in the land of the living is nearly impossible. One feels swallowed whole by the darkness. Suffocated. Trying to wade through the endless blackness, especially entirely alone, as I did, is like slogging through the worst, infested swamp and deepest sludge imaginable. It is exhausting. It surely does not seem worth the effort.

Where does all this pain come from? It is created by having "felt needs" that remain unmet. The hopelessness that these cravings and their lack of fulfillment create leave us in despair: we either need our pain to cease or a loss of consciousness. When it becomes apparent that having these needs met is an impossibility it can feel like the bottom has dropped out of our insides. All is lost, but most especially we are lost. But it is not our situation alone that constitutes our crises. Rather it is our life-dominating desire that is interpreting our situation that turns the loss of the realization of felt needs into hopelessness and then plunges us into suicide.

God means for these idols to bring us up empty. He insists that He is the only thing worth that degree of focus or worship. That only a deep, abiding relationship with Him will really fill the depths of those needs. The hole, He insists, is God-shaped and He is the only God that will fit into it perfectly. Everything else will come up short. If you find the strength and the courage to turn from your broken dreams to embrace His offer He will remind you that Christ has risen and overcome sin (including our idolatry), death (including our emotional and spiritual states), and the grave (the only place we want to be at that moment).

Psalm 33 is assuring. Verses 18 and 19 say, "Behold, the eye of the Lord is on those who fear Him, on those who hope in His mercy. To deliver their soul from death, and to keep them alive in famine." Sometimes it is the famine of the soul that matters the most. And that is an appetite that God means for us to have satisfied in Him alone.

There are many examples of people who, throughout Scripture, suffered greatly. The Psalms are chock-full of examples of people who were depressed and yet most overcame by shifting their hopeless thoughts about their circumstances to hope-filled thoughts about Who God is and the faithfulness of His character. The Psalms of David are good examples. In the New

Testament, Paul gives us hope repeatedly by the things that he endured in suffering and overcame by God's grace. There are numerous examples of church martyrs throughout modern history - including the present day - that demonstrate the faithfulness of God and the victory of those who put their trust in God, despite the circumstances.

Many people can testify that through their darkest hours they could feel the very presence of God. I cannot testify of this. In my darkest hours I felt that God had forgotten me or abandoned me and this greatly intensified my suffering. Scripture, of course, states emphatically that God never leaves us or forsakes us (Matthew 28:20). We have to believe it by faith. But that does not mean that it never feels like He has left us. Faith is tested in the fire. And this is when we find out what we really believe... What we really love...What we really worship. And, after all, maybe that is why God has sent the trial: to test our faith (1 Peter 1:6-9).

It is in this very testing that we must learn to live by faith, to stake our all on the Word of God and His faithfulness to His promises, and the rock-solid dependability of His attributes. And in that fledgling faith we must cry out to Him, knowing that He hears us, and bring our hurts to Him. He could have prevented them all and yet required that we go through these dark hours. Maybe they were the consequences of our own mistakes and hence constitute our consequences. Maybe they were the direct fault of others who sinned against us. Perhaps they were acts of God. Whatever the situation, we have to learn to trust that He has a purpose, even when there is no way to see it from our vantage point.

It is by faith that the apostle Paul stated that our present sufferings are not worth comparing with the glory that will be revealed in our eternal state (Romans 8:18). Paul's own monumental sufferings are partially recorded in Scripture and demonstrate the power of Paul's faith in God to greatly reward those who endure hardship as a good soldier of the cross.

The truth is, however, that apart from faith in Christ, our lives seem to have no purpose in our suffering. Over and over again we look in vain for why these terrible things happened to us, why it keeps coming, and never seem to be able to adequately resolve the questions within ourselves. Some of these questions are addressed in the chapter about suffering and slowly brought out over months of working with the process. I have personally discovered many scripts and broadcast messages that I have had most of my life that are wholly negative and have been contributing factors in my life's struggles. As I slowly work to eliminate them, the response of the world around me *to me* has become increasingly positive. And this is precisely why I have included the information in the book. Please understand that the information from Dr. Bradley Nelson is as helpful to me personally and spiritually, as have been the biblical principles contained in this book. What is shared by Dr. Nelson has been healing and has greatly aided my spiritual growth.

Please remember that our greatest hope is in Christ and His resurrection. Because He lives our hope is real. Hope, biblically defined, is not some optimistic, vague wish that things would be a certain way, but is an absolute confidence that what He said is true. Our real hope is not dependent upon anyone other than Christ. Because our hope was accomplished by the power of God, and is kept by the power of God, nothing can take it or destroy it. Nothing can get to us except by the predetermined will of God. Thus, we can trust He sent our suffering to accomplish His purposes.

This book, written after a lifetime of intense, and often unbearable suffering, is my testimony to these things. While immersed in the hemorrhaging of my life, of my very spirit, I have struggled beyond measure to justify my suffering, my pain... my existence. Why go on living at all? This [suffering] never ends! I would end it! I am sick and tired of it! What the_____ is this for? What *is* the purpose?

While no one should justify their sins against another person based upon something good eventually coming out of the other person's suffering (this has been done in my life, most notably by my parents), it is nevertheless our own responsibility to make something good out of the diarrhea vomited on us if at all possible. Someone once said, "If life hands you lemons, make lemonade." I have to agree!

When we have Christ, we have a living hope that our struggles will yet materialize for good in His grand purposes (Romans 8:28,29). And Peter said that we have "an inheritance that can never perish, spoil or fade" (1 Peter 1:4). With this living hope in a living God, with a living Savior that has been tried and tested by the same things that we face (Isaiah 53; Hebrews 11:2-3), what we achieve with our lives (i.e. our eternal inheritance stored up in heaven for us) won't be destroyed, broken into by thieves or ruined by our troubles, trials or circumstances. It will be there waiting for us when God takes us home.

The fact of this indestructible inheritance is set off by the apostle Paul in 2 Corinthians 4 where he shares some of the struggles that he endured while working to share the gospel. After some details of those struggles, in verse 17, he refers to them as "light and momentary afflictions." How's that, Paul? They surely don't seem light and momentary down here! As he points out in verses 10-12 and 15, his whole life was lived with purpose. He understood that his sufferings had purpose in redemptive history. His whole life, as he saw it, was related to the future reward that he would be receiving from a Savior that was beyond reckoning here on earth (verses 17-18). He could describe his afflictions as "light" (bearable) and "momentary" (livable) when he considered the eternal reward that was awaiting him as a result of how he bore his sufferings here on earth.

In verse 16, Paul intimates that he is living his life daily by the renewal of the Holy Spirit, as should each of us. Being renewed is about being empowered to live life by the strength of God, an enabling to do God's work and God's will His way. It involves the capacity to endure the trials that come as a result of suffering for Christ's sake. Philippians 3:10 says, "I want to know [Christ] and the power of His resurrection and the fellowship of His sufferings, being conformed to His death." This means that Paul does not despair in his confusion about life's difficulties and he does not view his persecutions as God abandoning him (see 2 Corinthians 4:8-9).

Paul's long view of his suffering, seeing it as having eternal value regardless of his comprehension of it, also means he does not see himself as a powerless victim and does not have a self-centered view of the situation.

Suicide victims usually have a self-centered view of life and of their struggles. They usually see themselves as powerless and their suffering as unbearable and never-ending except by death. Truth be told, there are sufferings here on earth that do not end until death comes. When these sufferings are viewed as needing to be escaped from, suicide becomes the dominate desire. This is especially true of those who live in horrific chronic physical pain. The thinking in such people becomes clouded by the pain and this is sometimes accompanied by pain medications or illicit drugs that further cloud the thinking. It can cause people to become self-absorbed and pre-occupied with the soon-to-be-an-idol desire for relief. This can easily morph into a desire to die if nothing else works or does not work well enough. The aggressiveness of our pain seems only matched by the aggressiveness of a suicidal act of desperation.

Common Suicidal Risk Factors

If you or someone you love is potentially at risk for suicide the following are common indicators of risk:

Extreme psychological pain related to unmet psychological needs.
A view of self that says she cannot tolerate such intense pain.
An overwhelming feeling of hopelessness, and the belief that she is helpless to solve problems.

A sense of isolation or desertion accompanied by the belief that others cannot, should not, or do not want to offer support, nurture, or care.

A repetitive thought that ending life is the only way to escape the pain or the problem.[25]

While these can also describe someone who is depressed, they can be more intense in those with PTSD or those who are suicidal. Always bear in mind that those who are suicidal are also depressed, among other things. And suicide is an interplay among all these variables. Jeffery Black gives the example of a sense of hopelessness, combined with a pattern of poor coping, a limited tolerance for pain, and a flight from help can combine to encourage someone to plan a suicide. Furthermore, hopelessness can be a cause of psychological problems and a result of other psychological issues. There is also a strong link between someone feeling powerless and viewing the situation as unchangeable. Add to this the inability to bear prolonged and intense pain.[26]

If you are feeling suicidal try to discern what thwarted felt need is being associated in your mind with this problem. If you have come to believe that you cannot endure the pain associated with that unmet need you will feel hopeless and will likely view your-

---

25 These were five points were taken from Black's *Suicide. Understanding and Intervening* _p. 11.

26 Again, I cannot overstate the value here of Dr. Nelson's emotional release therapy covered in a later chapter. Before attempting suicide, everyone who finds life this difficult and can only be preoccupied with a desire to die should try his approach. It has brought emotional and psychological healing to scores of people, the author included.

self or your situation as unchangeable. Is this accurate? Ask for counsel and read the Word of God to find the answers. Be honest with yourself.

My belief that life was not worth living if I could not escape the combination of my physical and emotional and psychological pain, or if my dream did not come true, was not God's view of the situation. Trying to adjust my thinking to grasp that God had a different plan was deeply distressing. My conviction that my plan was better than His was grounded in my experience and the sin of pride, not trust of Him or His plans or His purposes.

Hopelessness is an indicator that our thinking is not biblical. It may indicate a lack of godly wisdom. We need to bring our thinking processes in line with God's Word. Faith involves a belief in God's goodness and wisdom and that He can be trusted with respect to these factors in our lives as well. What we discover when we are hopeless is the depth of our faith in God and the depth of our theology. Do we really know Him? Do we really know the Word? Do we really believe either?

Hopelessness is a result of desiring things here on earth more than what God wants for us. When we do not trust what He wants for us we become hopeless. Frustration follows. After all, God thwarted our plans to pursue our own desires, our idols. It can be extremely difficult to die to these desires but Christ is our example. While praying in the Garden of Gethsemane He bowed His will to that of the Father and prayed, "Yet not my will be done but Thine." Sometimes letting go of those idols is costly, and sometimes they were not idols but nevertheless to let them go is still painful. It can be a natural thing that grief or the grieving process ensues from these losses.

If we are looking for our reward here on earth then we will be disappointed for where our treasure is where our heart will be. If we are storing up our eternal treasure where nothing can get to it or destroy it then we will not only have hope but joy. Our losses will look much smaller, though they are still very real losses. Nevertheless, we must shift our focus from things of the earth to eternal things.

When we allow our felt needs to be what motivates us rather than a desire to live to please God, then we will perceive some things as needs that are only deeply held desires. The failure of a marriage is tragic, yes, but if you are left by a spouse, as painful as that is, dying is not necessary, no matter how much we desire it. We cannot fail to recognize our sinfulness when we skew our thinking out of alignment with God's. The skewing of our thoughts out of alignment with truth will only increase our pain and disappointments.

If We Would Help

Depression and suicidal tendencies can be very wearing on anyone, including on those around them. If you believe that a suicide is immanent then please call 911 and have the person admitted for care immediately. The Veteran's Administration has a suicide prevention hotline that is nationwide. Take seriously the threats, the hopelessness, the despair that is expressed to you. The loss of one's temper in an abusive explosion may make you feel better but it will not help the situation or your relationship with that person. What the person realizes is that it was a mistake to speak with you about the problem and it will prevent them from seeking help from you in the future, and possibly seeking any at all from anyone. But this type of response may be enough to put somebody over the edge; it may be the straw to break the camel's back.

Rather than responding selfishly to someone having such difficulty seeing past what overwhelms her, try something else. First, be sure that you validate the pain. Acknowledging that the person is experiencing great emotional or psychological pain is a comfort. Offer to help the person get medical care if possible. The need for someone to care, someone to empathize, increases in the crisis, not decreases. Acknowledgment of the person's suffering can ease the pain alone.

Secondly, we can try to help the person see the connection between the pain and the conflict in the perceived felt need. This should be done without immediately attacking the person theologically about this need constituting an idol of the heart. Kindness and gentleness can be very effective tools at helping someone change the point of view that is causing such hopelessness and a desire to end it all. If you can encourage the person to name the felt need it can help reveal it for what it is and this realization may bring it into sharper focus.

In talking with people about their situation it is okay to challenge what they are thinking and the ways that their thinking does not line up with reality or has contradictions in it. Be cautious to do so in love. Talk with them about what solutions they have tried in the past and what worked or didn't work. How do they define "worked" and "didn't work?" Was it realistic? Was it true? What is the person's definition of success? You may find that some people give up easily or attempted something that was out of his or her reach. Perhaps the goal was unrealistic or beyond his or her control to achieve in the first place. Some things should not be attempted without support or adequate training.

Jeffrey Black says that exploring someone's conceptions of what defines "hopeless" is also important.

> "Intellectually, hopelessness is the utter certainty that there is no solution to a problem, and the loss of what [s/h]e values is certain. [S/h]e sees no hope. Emotionally, hopelessness is a pervasive despair and misery, or dread of the future. [S/h]e feels no hope. Research shows that hopelessness is the single strongest predictor of suicide."[27]

Among those who consume alcohol heavily, the level of hopelessness expressed was the deciding factor in predicting suicide.[28] This was also true of those who abused drugs. In fact, it was better as a predictor in those situations than was the mea-

---

27 Black, *Suicide. Understanding and Intervening*, p. 21.

28 A. Beck, A. Weissman, & M. Kovacs, "Alcoholism, Hopelessness and Suicidal Behavior," *Journal of Studies on Alcohol*, 37(1), 1976.

sure of depression.[29] For those who are depressed it marked the difference between feeling very down and the person's suicidal intent.[30]

If you are trying to determine if someone is at risk for suicide please understand that contacting professionals, even if it is 911, is an option. It would be better to err on the side of safety and bring the person to the attention of authorities than allow the person to destroy him or her self.

Nevertheless, some guidelines can be offered. For the person you are trying to assess the suicidal risk of, the event is the reason. It is not necessarily all the other things that precipitated the depression and/or suicidal thoughts. It is what is here and now that has broken the person's desire to go on.

You may need to gather background information, depending upon how well you know the person. Has the person tried suicide before? How? When? Why? What coping skills does the person have? Does the person have a plan? Has s/he sought counseling for this problem before? Has there been a change in medications that increased suicide risk? Are there other medical problems? Etc.

Look at the person's substance use and abuse. While this is not always possible because they become good at hiding it, try to

---

29 G.D. Emery, R.A. Steer, and A. Beck, "Depression, Hopelessness & Suicidal Intent among Heroin Addicts," *International Journal of Addictions*, 16(3), 1981, pp. 425-429.

30 M. Kovacs, A. Beck, and A. Weissman, "Hopelessness: An Indicator of Suicidal Risk," *Suicide and Life-threatening Behavior* 5(2), 1975, pp. 98-103.

access whether or not there is an increase in vulnerability or dependency here. While we can not make a one-to-one correlation, they do often go hand-in-hand. The following may be indicators that can be used to determine the suicide risk in individuals:

Present involvement in drug or alcohol support groups

The person's length of abstinence or the length of time the person has been using (amounts generally increase over time and could escalate sharply to the point of accidental overdosing)

The present level of use, especially as compared to previous levels

The level of temptation to use as reported to you by the user

Drugs or alcohol already being used by a person as a coping mechanism should be of concern. S/he is already choosing to alter the state of consciousness in order to find relief. It is not much further to the step of suicide.

It must also be borne in mind that the habituation of drug or alcohol use exacerbates depression, mood swings and dependency that alters the behavior and consequently the relationships that these people are in.

It is not uncommon, for this reason, that people with PTSD either have everyone around them desert them or they find that they, themselves, will withdraw from people for emotional protection.

If you cannot be the person's support system, then try to contact people who can be resources. If the person's suffering level can be reduced even a little, it is possible that even this slightest improvement could cause them to choose life. Encouragement in this respect could be life-saving.

On the other hand, if the person has a definite plan, or has already obtained everything necessary to carry out the act, and has even planned against potential interruptions, or at worst, has already attempted a dry run then do not hesitate to act with haste. These are all indicators of genuine intent and should not be lightly dismissed.

When They Have Medicine Available

Millions of people who are depressed, if or when they reach out for help, will often times find themselves prescribed an antidepressant. They may also be taking pain medications, possibly narcotics. Add to the mix the problem of taking sleeping medication, and any other medications they are on. By the time all is counted, someone could be on a lethal combination of medications, some of which could be counteracting each other in organ-damaging ways.

Often times what happens is that the self-prescribed doses of medications increase, and eventually alcohol is added, and thus self-medicating becomes deadly, whether intentional or not. In such situations, it can be difficult to determine if someone's death was deliberate or accidental. Loved ones are often left wondering.

Medications are also used to escape not just the pain but life itself. Again, coupled with alcohol it can be not only habit-forming but deadly. The habituation of self-medicating makes it easier to increase the dose and to take that fatal dose that is just a little too far. More meds is not necessarily better, but that does not mean that we do not arrive at the faulty conclusion all the same. Neither does it keep us from trying to use the medications to escape.

The problems inherent in medicating can also lead to other complications in life. Unemployment due to drug or alcohol use is not uncommon. Those with PTSD already have difficulty holding it together. Add the complications of medications and their side effects and it can be exacerbated, sometimes greatly. These attendant stressors can lead to even more stressors: financial problems, relational problems, more health problems, public disgrace or exposure, even the possibility of immoral or illegal allegations or charges. These types of problems often lead to an increase in drug or alcohol use, especially as sleeplessness increases, or depression is exacerbated. A vicious cycle commences that destroys the user and the lives of those around them.

Monitoring these medications may become an important step in being prepared for what someone with PTSD will do. Perhaps contacting the family doctor or primary care provider would be wise. Track how often the prescription is refilled. Monitor it yourself. If the prescribed dosage is adhered to than many harmful side-effects and addictions can be avoided. Increasing the dose without the doctor's permission is unwise and can lead to devastating problems. Beware.

If Someone You Love Committed Suicide

It is possible that you have picked up this book because someone you loved has or had PTSD and you are hoping to gain more understanding. Because the suicide rate for those with PTSD is astronomical this is a life-threatening problem.[31] At least 18 veterans every day commit suicide from PTSD. And that does not include the general population's numbers. It is a real problem.

When people commit suicide they leave in the ensuing debris that was their life, a sea of unanswered questions that usually haunt the survivors who had loved them for the rest of their lives. There are a sea of emotions that rip through, feelings so intense that they can feel like physical pain. Confusion, disorientation, anger, betrayal, guilt, or a sense of failed responsibility or even the fear of doing the same thing themselves.

Once again there is a need to pursue this path of grief and suffering in faith. Deuteronomy 29:29 says, "The secret things belong to the Lord our God, but the things revealed belong to us and to our children forever, that we may follow all the words of this law." Following God's Word in faith will aide our grieving process and help us find peace in His Truth. The truth will set us free.

---

31 To highlight the severity of the problem see Time's March 7, 2011 issue and the article A Soldier's Tragedy by Mark Thompson or Penny Coleman's book Flashback. Posttraumatic Stress Disorder, Suicide and the Lessons of War.

We will likely never have the majority of our questions answered in the wake of someone's suicide but we can trust that God has the matter firmly in hand. It is that relationship with God that can bring you peace, not having all of the answers to your questions. You will never have the answer to all the loose ends that you are trying to tie up. You will never feel "good" about this nor the suicide. You may very well never fully recover from your loss, or the shock of your discovery of the person's death.

The only thing that we can really do in a crisis like this is turn to God. John 6.68-69 records Peter speaking to Christ, saying, "Lord, to whom shall we go? You have the words of eternal life. We believe and know that you are the Holy One of God." Only God will be bigger than your pain, your distress, your sorrow and broken heartedness. Bringing it to Him will not hurt Him nor overburden Him. He is big enough to handle all of it. At some very fundamental level we finally have to acknowledge that we may never really struggle through to a full resolution but that we can leave it with God. Come to Him and cling to Him. He will not let you go. Christ came to earth as a man to suffer the same afflictions that are common to humanity (Isaiah 53; Hebrews 2:17-18). He knows what it is to grieve the death of someone you love (John 11).

God never promised us that we would have a happy life, a life free of suffering or difficulty. But He does promise that our afflictions will not be able to separate us from the love of God in Christ Jesus our Lord (Romans 8). We can cling to these promises and cling to Him in our suffering. Dive into the Scriptures and find expression in the words of the psalmists who brought their great pain to God and poured out their lament to Him. He will not be offended.

One very important thing to do at this time is to connect with other people. Do not try to walk through these matters alone. Gather with others who have been affected by this suicide or by the plight of someone else who committed suicide. You not only don't have to avoid discussing it, but you shouldn't avoid it. You may find yourself able to bond more closely at such a time with those who understand. Come together to grieve; this is the opposite message of the loneliness and isolation that is intrinsically a part of suicide.

If we respond rightly to the situation it does not have to destroy us. It can bring people together in deeper, more lasting relationships with others. This could be a precious gift that is left in the wake of disaster. Use it to your own advantage.

You yourself may currently be considering suicide in the aftermath of another suicide. Rather than pursuing it, endeavor to live a fruitful life. Don't neglect getting up in the morning, personal hygiene, duties and responsibilities, or just normal living. God can work in you and through you to be a channel of blessing to others who are living with the same burden. If you will respond to others with gentleness and compassion in their suffering rather than a hardened, toxic heart, then you will find that you are able to comfort others with the comfort that you yourself have received from God. Good *can* come from your suffering, from your loved one's death. Be encouraged.

The Perishing Mindset Of PTSD

What we go through

What is meant by "the perishing mindset?" This perishing mindset is the mentality of those who are lost and without Christ in this world (Ephesians 2:11, 12). It is a futile way of thinking (Romans 1:21; 1 Corinthians 3:20; Ephesians 4:17-19). When this mentality continues to prevail in the thinking of a believer they are said to have the "perishing mentality". They are commonly depressed and in despair, without hope and overwhelmed by difficulties. They may have largely given up on life and on themselves. And they've given up on God; they do not seek Him and do not worship Him. They are being ruled by their emotions and not the precepts of Scripture.

People who find themselves making decisions based upon their emotions, rather than biblical precepts, will be tossed to and fro with every new bit of information that comes to them. They often times dwell on bitterness and self-pity. They wreak of disappointment and discontent. They tend to be unforgiving and yet want the forgiveness they feel entitled to for their petty grievances. They also tend to have a great deal of emotional pain balled up inside of them, often as a result of their own sin. This often results in a very lonely life. So what is the solution? Where do we begin?

How we heal Biblically

Renewing the Mind

Renewing the mind is the process of becoming so familiar with the Word of God and the knowledge of the Holy One Himself that we begin to be pre-occupied with being like Him and having our thoughts dwell upon Him. It is hard work, to be sure. It is essential because you become like the thing that you think upon. If your focus is violence on a screen, then you will become likened to it. If you pursue peaceful things, lovely things, you will become likened to that. Hence, if you think about God, you will become like Him. This is the goal of renewing the mind.

It requires that the learner have a humble, teachable spirit and a genuine desire to understand what God says is required of you in order for you to change into the godly person He meant for you to be. It will most definitely require a steadfast commitment to change. Only after committing to change will real, sustained heart and lifelong change take place; your motives, thoughts and desires must be changed at a fundamental level for victory over the perishing mindset to become a way of life. Your mind is a battlefield and it must come to hate that which you once loved that was not godly. It is an act of the will.[32]

The main theological passage that directs us to renew our minds is Romans 12:1 & 2. Please also see 2 Corinthians 10:5, Psalm 119, and Philippians 4:8. There are many more of these jewels in the Bible and, as you explore its riches, you will find your own precious stones with which to build your thinking in new and lasting ways.

We deliberately set out to renew our minds; it does not happen by accident. We do so by faithfully reading Scripture, studying it and memorizing it. Sitting under the teaching of an able preacher of the Word will be of immense value. When temptations come, pull out the arsenal of spiritual weaponry that you have acquired to fight that specific temptation. Quote that truth out loud if you can, but surely rehearse it in your mind. Do this as long as you have to in order to gain victory over your temptation.

The process of renewing the mind is learned over time through repetition and dedication. The benefit of having a mentor cannot be overstated. But in the absence of a mentor, a Christian still has the Lord, hopefully a copy of the Scriptures, and the Holy Spirit. Pray for a Christian friend who will help you walk in the newness of life that God has saved you for.

---

32 Several books can be recommended for this battle of the mind. Mark Shaw's The Heart of Addiction, Elizabeth Elliot's Loving God with all Your Mind, and John Vandegriff's In the Arena of the Mind.

Begin by committing yourself to the knowledge that we must be living our lives by principle, and not by emotions. We must learn to think before we act or before we speak. It is necessary for us to invest ourselves into learning and knowing the Word of God, its commands, and its practical applications. This will require that a solid, biblical mentor be found for the purposes of teaching you how to read and study Scripture with the intent that you will be changed by it and be conformed to the image of Christ because of it. There are no shortcuts to this procedure. It will take hours of time used constructively and consistently for the glory of God. But obedience to the will and Word of God is absolutely critical to the healing process for those with PTSD.

Bitterness

Bitterness is often a life-dominating sin of people who have suffered traumas (Job 7:11, 9:18, 10:1, 21:25; Proverbs 14:10; Isaiah 38:15-17; Lamentations 3:5, 15; Ezekiel 27:31; Acts 8:23; Romans 3:14; Ephesians 4:31; Hebrews 12:15). They may be tender-hearted towards others who are not close to them or tender towards general causes. But around those that are close to them, they are selfish indeed.

Bitter people tend to be the best critics of themselves, especially when they are sober. They are often times extremely critical of those who hurt them and reject them, possibly perceiving a wound where there was none. Being prone to bitterness already, usually results in more bitterness creeping into the heart. They will eventually become rebellious if wounds accumulate over time, especially against a specific person or regarding a specific situation. They will eventually develop crushed spirit (Proverbs 18:14). A crushed spirit is the feeling of hurt and rejection that results from being hurt. It can seem unbearable, especially to someone who is overly sensitive and inventive regarding imagined or perceived hurts.

Bitter people replay the memories of the people who hurt them, or the situations in which they were hurt. They keep their wounds fresh. When this seed of pain is continually brought to remembrance it becomes bitterness. This bitterness, when given the cultivated ground of a proud heart, will spring up eternal. In other words, it would take a great deal of sanctification for the person to move into the realm of forgiving, which is the antidote to bitterness.

Hebrews 12:15 states, "looking carefully lest anyone fall short of the grace of God; lest any root of bitterness springing up cause trouble, and by this many become defiled." The life-dominating sin of bitterness truly goes out in damaging ripples to all those it touches. Women, in particular, tear down their own homes with their own hands (Proverbs 14:1). Bitter people seek revenge that can destroy not only their intended targets but also themselves.

Matthew 6:9-15 is the Lord's prayer. It emphasizes that we must be as forgiving of others as we want God to be of us and our transgressions. Genesis 50:17 speaks of the need of families to be forgiving within families and is an excellent example for all of us to live by. Matthew 18:21-35 reminds us that we must be willing to forgive anyone, whatever trespasses s/he has committed, every time that the person repents and seeks forgiveness. As hard as this is to do, it is about the offended person being free from the bondage that results from unforgiveness. It impairs our relationships, most notably with God. It also, therefore, hinders our prayers and our spiritual growth. As our spiritual growth is hindered, we are prevented from obtaining the natural growth that comes from an increase in the wisdom and knowledge of God. The costs of bitterness are not worth what we get in return for letting it go: moral freedom.

Self-pity

Self-pity is at the root of the perishing mentality. It serves as the driving energy that fuels a mind that has entered despair. It is based in the life-dominating sin of pride. It says, "I deserve better than this." Or, "I don't deserve this _____." This is the world's current belief, made prolific by the godless self-esteem movement.[33] The pride behind this view of one's life fixes its gaze upon an unrealistic expectation that life should have been different, or better. "Life *should* have treated *me* better." This view says that the poor wretch has knowledge and insight into his or her life that is superior in understanding and wisdom to God's wisdom. It is steeped in discontent and self-absorption. It is an all-pervasive mindset of selfish preoccupation. It is toxic. It must be repented of and abandoned. It has to be replaced with thoughts that dwell upon God and acknowledge the sovereignty of God and the mysteries of His choices. His ways are not our

---

33 Please see Jay Adam's book on the subject, The Biblical View of Self-Esteem, Self-Love & Self-Image, by Harvest House Publishers.

ways (Isaiah 55:8, 9). They are higher, regardless of what we do or do not understand about them. When they do not make sense to us, we must humbly acknowledge that He knows and understands more than we do. And bow our knees to the greatness of the magnitude of His wisdom.

Discontentment and Disappointments

This settled attitude of discontentment is typical of the perishing mindset. There is a distinct belief that somehow things should be better and the place where God has stationed this person is beneath him or her. This goes hand in hand with the self-pity that dominates the person. The outlook is an established pessimism that has a lock upon the brain and everything filters through that negative grid on its way in and out.

The mind of a believer is suppose to use the Scriptures for a filter. The Word of God is literally suppose to act as a sieve in the mind, immediately identifying truth from error, good from bad. For the discontented person, the grid of negativity replaces the Scriptures for the most part. If the Scriptures are at all a part of this person's thinking, it is sandwiched between two grids of negativity so that the most negative slant can be put on both the incoming and outgoing messages. This toxicity makes this person difficult to bear.

These people are disappointed in life in almost every way. They conclude that God must hate them for life to be this bad. Life's venue is horrible and its offerings to this person are stale and tasteless, especially when seeing the wonderful things that God has given others. The Smith vs. The Jones mentality of comparing his life to others' lives is entrenched, and feeds this discontentment, and the self-pity cycle.

The "if only" set in and this person thinks that "if only I had _____, then everything would be better." "If only I was _____, I would be happy." "Everyone else has _____. Why don't I?" This defeatist attitude and the jealousy of others' things and their lives only destroys people by contributing so greatly to their toxicity that ultimately no one can stand them... Then the loneliness sets in,... and they go deeper into the cycle of thinking that it is life, that it is everyone else and never themselves, which is the central problem.

These life-dominating, life and relationship destroying sins, must be repented of and the truth put on in place of these destructive mindsets. Unless God's Word becomes the regulator of their thoughts, they have no hope of overcoming the destructive mindset. This change of mental focus and the total revamping of thought processes will require perseverance and commitment to ever see any long-term change.

Contentment is learned. See Paul's reflections upon it in Philippians 4. It requires hard work to replace these toxic thoughts with thoughts of gratitude and praise to God for anything good, especially Who He is. Look for the blessings and see things as such rather than calling them curses. Paul's example in Philippians 1 about the different motives that people have for preaching the gospel was that, regardless of whether they did it for themselves and their own glory, or for the right motives, the gospel was preached, and for this he rejoiced and continued to rejoice. If we can get the same attitude, we can overcome our pessimism and glorify God in the midst of our tribulation. This change in us would demonstrate our salvation to those who know us and provide avenues of preaching the gospel that might otherwise never exist.

What Does Victory Over the Perishing Mindset Look Like?

What do you look for in yourself to encourage yourself regarding biblical change? One of the first things will be the joy in your life, along with a grateful spirit. You will also begin to develop a more caring and submissive spirit. If you are coming from the arena of addictions, for example, then you will also begin to be more responsible for your actions. Responsibility is critical to the process of transformation. It demonstrates that a change of heart has genuinely occurred. The transparency that develops in the life of someone who is now walking rightly will be a testament to the saving grace of God in your life. It testifies of Christ. You will also begin focusing upon others, you will more naturally serve others and be more giving to them. It is the heart of God to think of us and to give to us. Being like Him naturally means that His interests become our interests.

Rest assured of one thing: your transformation will be evident to everyone who knows you. They almost surely will say something to you and they will likely respond to you differently. Give God the glory for the great things He is doing!

Addictions

What we go through

Of all the topics included in this book about PTSD, this is the one thing about which I do not write from experience. God, in His infinite mercy, has spared me the seeking of refuge in drugs and alcohol. While I rarely drink alcohol or use narcotics, I do have them. Slavery to them has never been a problem. So this chapter has been researched even more than others. I sincerely hope it does not diminish the suffering people experience when facing this struggle.

The issue of addictions is not so much a part of PTSD per se as it is a coping mechanism for those who have PTSD. The desperate need to escape from the many challenges inherent in the disorder causes people to seek relief in many forms. Doctors tend to use medication, some of which are addicting, to help us balance our thoughts or aide us in sleeping. Yet they can become addicting in some cases. Most notably are the narcotic pain killers, for the many wounds of life and service, and the sleeping medications that are needed to just get to sleep. But often times these medications are turned to relief ever-increasingly and a desire for yet more relief is created, and eventually pursued. Unless this tendency is checked desperation will go overboard sooner or later. Add in the complication of alcohol as a drug intensifier and it can become a lethal combination.

God has answers for these issues, many of which is in the chapter on the emotion code. Some answers do not come that easily. Some will become a life-long struggle. But even these horrible struggles can be used by God - sometimes especially these struggles - to make us like His dear Son. In other words, they can be used as stepping stones for personal growth. In Christian terminology it is called progressive sanctification, the process of increasing in Christlikeness through growth in the wisdom and knowledge of God. As we struggle, sometimes daily, with our demons, we can use them to drive us to God to search for answers. Let us proceed then, to examine Scripture for insights and solutions to these problems.

A Biblical Depiction of Intoxication

Scripture shows us not only who we really are, but also clearly portrays the characters that play on its pages. Drunkenness is no exception to the rule. Two notable characters whose drunkenness is recorded are Noah and Lot (Genesis 9:20-27; Genesis 19:30-38).

Drunkenness leads to deep suffering, most notably crimes of violence that the drunkard either commits in this intoxicated state or is unable to defend his or herself against due to the alcohol. It leads to many other consequences, too, none of which are a blessing, including poverty of character, relationships and finances.

A significant passage in the Old Testament book of wisdom, Proverbs, tells us of the variety of troubles that come upon those who are drunk. Proverbs 23:29-35 says,

> "Who has woe? Who has sorrow? Who has contentions? Who has complaints? Who has wounds without cause? Who has redness of eyes? Those who linger long at the wine, those who go in search of mixed wine. Do not look on the wine

when it is red, When it sparkles in the cup, When it swirls around smoothly; at the last it bites like a serpent, and stings like a viper. Your eyes will see strange things, and your heart will utter perverse things. Yes, you will be like one who lies down in the midst of the sea, or like one who lies at the top of the mast, saying: 'They have struck me, but I was not hurt; They have beaten me, but I did not feel it. When shall I awake, that I may seek another drink?'"

These things describe anyone who is drunk. The absence of the use of the word "drunkard" being ascribed to this person is notable. This is not intended to refer solely to someone who has habituated drunkenness but also to anyone who gets drunk, period, regardless of how often.

The rhetorical questions asked in Proverbs obviously are answered, "By the one who is drunk." Many people drink to forget, to escape or to find what they believe will be pleasure. But this only leads to more problems. Biblically speaking, this person is a fool and is not a wise sage.

Wounds without cause refers to the many injuries that people awaken with, often times without even being able to remember where or how they got them. Being too inebriated to walk and falling into things can cause bumps, bruises and other problems that lead to "wounds without cause."

They also have a redness in their eyes. While this could surely be due to the consumption of the alcohol, it may also be from crying as a result of the sorrows that they have inflicted in their own lives. Many drinkers have sorrowful eyes regardless of the level of drunkenness or sobriety. Sin has its consequences and takes its toll.

We are admonished not to look at the wine when it is in the cup and sparkles and tempts us. Don't even look at it! For many, by the time that they get to this point, it is too great of a temptation to walk away from. Our hearts are tempted and drawn away by our own lusts, not really by the object of our lusts (James 1:13-15). The phrase to "look upon the wine" means to have our thoughts dwell upon the object of our desire. What we think upon will dictate what we do and the emotions that we experience. We must take our thoughts captive to our wills and the Spirit of God and make them obedient to God's Word (2 Corinthians 10:4-6).

The sting of an adder is the idea of a poisonous snake biting and leaving one dead or on the verge of death. This can be the effect of intoxication. If you do not die physically you may still contract many serious and long-term health problems. And there are legal ramifications that sting us in many ways as well.

Being under the control of an intoxicating substance can influence us to behave in ways that we would not conduct ourselves if we were sober. We can see strange things (hallucinations) and we can say perverse things that reveal the utter wickedness of our hearts' deepest, darkest recesses. People find out who you really are when you are drunk! Personal restraints and self-control are gone. This is the opposite of being controlled by the Holy Spirit whose fruit includes self-control.

This lack of self-control feels like someone who is on the most topsy-turvy portion of a ship, the mast, while it is being tossed in a storm on the waves. In this state, you will not even know it if someone strikes you or even sexually assaults you. Yet, despite these negatives, people imagine that there is so much enjoyment from what they are doing that they will say, "May I have another drink?" The Bible calls this foolishness.

How we heal Biblically

The Core Issue of Addictions

Many people today have been inundated by the worldview that addictions are diseases, which means that it isn't the addict's fault. Yet, sadly, this concept is no where found in Scripture.[34] This model, originally used by Bill Wilson, who founded Alcoholics Anonymous (AA), was taken from Scripture where it is a euphemism for "sin" (Psalm 102:3). It has since been transformed by secular usage to mean a disease in the strictest medical sense. This is incorrect. If we had a disease than it would not have been our fault and would not have required Christ's death on the cross. But He died to cover our *sin,* which is vitally important to remember because only sinners need a Savior and we are responsible for each instance of drug or alcohol usage of which we have been willing participants.

The real problem at the core of any addiction is idolatry. An idol of the heart is anything we are willing to sin to get, to have or to keep. For example, if you are willing to lie or cheat or embezzle to get money because you love money so much, then

---

34 Colossians 2.8: "See to it that no one takes you captive by philosophy and empty deceit, according to human tradition, according to the elemental spirits of the world, and not according to Christ."

it is an idol of the heart. Generally speaking, we believe that our idols will provide for us something that neither God nor anything else possibly can. We believe we need it more than anything and that it will make everything okay if we just get that thing. Most are willing to sin to obtain their idols, and others actually rise to the level of being willing to commit crimes to possess them.

However, no idol ever satisfies like an abundant spiritual relationship with God does. To the unbelieving this sounds preposterous. First Corinthians 2:14 tells us that the natural man i.e., the unsaved person, does not receive the things of God because the things of God are foolishness to those who are perishing. The so-called "perishing" are those who, due to unbelief in Christ, are condemned to hell already, so that someone would think it's ridiculous that the abundant life would be found in the person and finished work of Christ and living life to the glory of God, is not surprising in the least!

God has created each of us to be worshippers. If we do not worship Him, we *will* worship something else, whether drugs, alcohol, money, power, or even ourselves. You *are* a worshipper.

Each person, according to Hebrews 12:1, is a potential addict. We all have a "besetting sin" that we struggle with. It is thought that God permits this to keep us humble and dependent upon Him for our daily grace to live a life pleasing to Him.

Biblically speaking, addictions are addressed most significantly in two ways. First of all, we have the potential for addiction because we have been born sinners. The primary sin of addicts regarding substance abuse is idolatry. Idolatry is a very prevalent and significant sin choice because every time we choose something other than God to solve our problems we have chosen idolatrously and have sinned against God. Everyone does this each day on earth, and all of it is rooted in the sin of pride.

The second manner in which addiction is addressed is under the heading of "drunkenness" and refers to the effect that a drug has on the one who consumes it, no matter what it is. Whether the mode of ingestion is snorting, shooting, inhaling, or whatever, we are taking drugs or alcohol to alter the way we feel. When this approach to managing our life's situations is habituated, then we can be termed "addicted." So addiction, therefore, can be defined as "the persistent habitual use of a substance known by the user to be harmful."[35] These substances can produce physical dependence, but do not always do so. Physical dependency is determined by the substance in use and the body's chemistry; not all drugs work for people equally.

In the Bible God does not differentiate those who use alcohol to become intoxicated from those who use pills or powders or something else. They all fall under the heading of drunkenness. Abusers are not distinguished from those who are physically dependent. Drunkenness is the name of the condition and it is a problem of the heart. If you try to split hairs about whether you are buzzed versus drunk, then you have missed the point. Efforts

---

35 Shaw, Mark, *The Heart of Addiction. A Biblical Perspective*, p. ix of the Introduction.

to rationalize or justify your usage is a matter of allowing your pride to indulge your disobedience to God and minimize your wicked motives. You are right back where you were before: using.

Another term used is "abuse." I will define it as the "improper or excessive usage of some intoxicating substance that does not usually result in the physical dependency that habituation does." However, abusers can quickly become addicts if occasional usage becomes regular usage.

It is important to note that all substance abuse or excess use is sin. Mark Shaw states it this way:

"Excessive use of a substance is not just a simple sin problem. It is a life-dominating and life-devastating sin nature
problem. This sin nature problem requires the Savior's forgiveness and the Holy Spirit's power to overcome it; not just
an individual's 'will power.' It is the 'will of God power'
that overcomes addiction. The 'perishing' mentality fueled by pride, selfishness, and self-pity must be put-off. The
mind must be renewed by the Holy Spirit who works in con-
junction with God's Word under the authority of the local
church. A 'joyful' and optimistic mentality fueled by serving
and pleasing God (and others) must be 'put-on' to replace old
attitudes, thoughts and behaviors. It will require a change
in thinking and acting called 'repentance' to overcome your
substance abuse problems."[36]

---

36 Shaw, Mark, The Heart of Addiction. A Biblical Perspective, p. x of the Introduction.

What must be understood in order to be victorious over the sin of addiction is that it is an outward symptom of a much deeper spiritual problem. Therefore, it is not enough to just quit using drugs or alcohol. The addict will replace that addiction with another addiction unless there is a significant change of heart. The world calls this an "addictive personality." Transferring your addiction from chemical substances to another indulgence such as guns, computers, cameras, skiing, etc. will not in any way solve the heart issues underlying the idolatry. Without a significant change of heart there will be no real change at all.[37] The Bible teaches that it is out of the heart of man that proceeds all the issues of life (Matthew 15:18, 19). It is out of the overflow of the heart that the mouth speaks (Matthew 12:4). As a man thinks in his heart so is he (Proverbs 23:7). Therefore, he heart is *the* target that must be nailed for long-term, effectual change in the life of an addict.

The secular programs for substance abuse and addictions are man-centered and thus their goal is upon pleasing people first and foremost. This is not the best focus. The best focus would be on pleasing God and therefore a truly biblical focus will have Christ as the center of the program and not ourselves, or anyone

---

37 The heart, biblically defined, is not the cardiac pump in your chest. It is the mind, the will and the emotions of a person. What we think on determines what we do, which in turn directly affects our emotions. If God becomes the focus of your thoughts you can not only sanctify your emotions through this process but also change the motivations behind your actions. This in turn will change your behaviors. You will live right when you think right. Hence renewing the mind with the Word of God is essential in dealing with addictions.

else. Indeed, living in the fear of man and the opinions of others is another idol! We have made no progress at all if we replace one idol with another when deciding whether we will or will not use drugs. Our purpose in overcoming the substances is to live a life of moral freedom[38] so that we can glorify God in all that we say and do.

The changes of heart that are necessary for long-term victory over idols of our hearts are only accomplished with the grace and help of God dwelling within us and changing what we want so that we want to do the right thing. In other words, God changes our willingness to be changed and He changes what we want! Our heart's desire is now for the things that please Him and not as much for the things that please our sinful desires. Now that is *real* change! Upon salvation God begins to replace our flawed, perishing mentality from when we were lost and separated from Him by our sin and our sin nature, with His joy and right thinking. He does this for a simple reason: we are in need of a complete transformation, not just recovery from drugs and alcohol usage. Our old selves are made new in Christ and we become new creations that have a second chance to get it right, which is truly an encouraging thought!

How is this done? The first step to being new is salvation. Secondly, we have to put off the old habits i.e., habituated idols, and be renewed in our minds by reading the Scriptures. Then

---

38 Moral freedom is freedom from life-dominating sins so that we are free to live our lives as we ought. Freedom is not about simply being able to do whatever we want but rather the moral "freeness" to do that which a godly person would do in obedience to the Word of God.

we have to adopt a godly habit to replace the old habit. If we do not replace the old habit with a righteous one, we will, sooner or later, fall right back into the old habits because we don't know what else to do!

The old habits of our sin nature do not simply disappear upon salvation. Our sin nature is not eradicated by coming into union with Jesus Christ. Therefore, there are new issues to face when an addict finds Christ.

One of those issues that requires change is behavior, namely one becomes obedient to God's commands by the convicting power of the Holy Spirit that now dwells within you. The Holy Spirit convicts you of guilt over your sin (John 16:8-11). When this conviction for sin comes, if you respond rightly, then God will use it to draw you to Himself for forgiveness. But when we respond wrongly, we become hardened by the deceitfulness of sin and we quench the Holy Spirit in our lives (Hebrews 3:13, 1 Thessalonians 5.:19).

Do You See Yourself as "Compulsive?"

Many addicts define themselves with the term "compulsive." But what does that terminology really say about a substance user? First of all, it implies that someone is unable to control the behavior, and this is usually not true. Something that is truly compulsive is irresistible in nature and must be performed, even if it is an irrational act. Substance use and abuse, however, are behaviors for which Scripture clearly delineates that we are personally responsible. Therefore, we are wrong to label an addict's behavior as compulsive; it would imply that it's biologically determined, or that even the Lord Himself could not stop someone from committing this behavior.

The term "compulsive" wrongly allows the addicted person to

Deny responsibility
Deny God's power to change them
Blame parents for poor upbringing as a child
Blame God for making them in this manner[39]

These behaviors have actually been repeated so often that we simply think of them in terms of compulsive. But they have been planned and executed so often that their habituation has actually rooted in our own thought system, and that translates to your heart.

In order to replace these habits we must change our thinking. We have to think in terms of righteous habits that are deliberately premeditated in the process of renewing the mind. In other words, we must replace sin habits by deciding in advance upon new, God-honoring conduct that conforms to the standards of Scripture. Armed with these new strategies and tactics, the next time that we encounter the same situations that tempt us to sin, we implement these new choices instead. Thereby we change the way we respond to situations that cause us to fall back into our old, sinful ways.

---

39 Shaw, *The Heart of Addiction*, p. 24.

This approach can be used with any sin that we are struggling against, for all of our sin choices ultimately can be defined as idols of the heart. Having a plan in advance is necessary for us to be ready to defeat the world, the flesh and the devil when they attack us anew.[40]

In addition to this approach is the timeless principle of sowing and reaping in Galatians 6:7-9. "Do not be deceived, God is not mocked; for whatever a man sows, that he will also reap. For he who sows to his flesh will of the flesh reap corruption, but he who sows to the Spirit will of the Spirit reap everlasting life. And let us not grow weary while doing good, for in due season we shall reap if we do not lose heart."

Addictions come as a result of sowing to our flesh, repeatedly, as a habit of life. If we live a life in the flesh and not one directed and governed by our spirit we reap death as a consequence. But if we sow to the spiritual side of our existence than we will reap eternal life. Simply put, a life lived for hedonistic pleasure will in the end result in a life destroyed. But a life that is lived to the glory of God will reap the benefits of good character, a good reputation and joy. The consequences, in every respect, of living for pleasure will catch up with you sooner or later. It is as much a spiritual law as an agricultural one.

In terms of addiction, it is a fact that satisfying our natural appetites will temporarily assuage them but it will be a strategy that,

---

40 1 John 2.16, 1 Peter 5.8

in the long run, is slavery to the very thing we thought would bring us joy or comfort.

There is a saying in Christendom that is surely true:

> Sin always takes you further than you wanted to go,
> It keeps you longer than you wanted to stay,
> And it costs you more than you wanted to pay.

Indeed, the cost of sin is always far greater than it appears at first blush. When King David took Uriah's wife, Bathsheba, in adultery the conception of a child was not on his mind, nor did he ever think that he would murder Uriah to cover it, along with 60 or more Israelites in the battle. Nor did he anticipate that the child would die at only a week of age. And he could not have imagined that his house would never have death or sexual sin leave it while he was living, nor that his sin would cause a division of the kingdom and a coup d'etat that would cost him both his kingdom and his son Absolom's life. Even Bathsheba's grandfather became so embittered against David that he joined the coup, and when the coup failed, he committed suicide. The fallout was staggering, to say the very least. And this is the way that sin goes for all of us.

These issues of addiction can only be healed as we address the heart issues of slavery. Breaking the bondage hold of sin is solely in the realm of the King of Kings and the Lord of Lords, Jesus Christ. It is also entirely possible that the substance abuse could cause demonic bondage,[41] and demonic bondage is also only broken by the power of Jesus Christ, Who triumphed over the demons on the cross (Colossians 2:15). Deliverance from all forms of sin bondage comes from Christ alone.

The problem in addictions is not first and foremost the substances being abused. Those are external matters. The issues are bound up in the heart of man, in the thoughts, intents and behaviors that we exhibit when we choose the substances. These fleshly and selfish desires challenge our desire to make better moral choices, and often times we succumb to the lure of the chemicals and the desires that well up inside of us.

Please understand that whatever effort you make to abandon any idol can only be done under the power of the Holy Spirit, which is yours only upon putting your faith in the person and work of Jesus Christ. Any other efforts, no matter how well intentioned, will fail because you are doing them in your own strength and not with the empowerment of God. The ability to be triumphant over your sin does not come from self-help because you really are unable to help yourself. The typical secular group programs, for example, tell you that you need a "higher power." But if you are the one choosing the "god" then how much higher

---

41 The original Greek manuscripts use the term "pharmakeia" to denote witchcraft and sorcery, purely demonic pursuits. This is where we derive our word pharmacy. The use of drugs and alcohol, even then, was associated with demonic spirits. The use of these substances opens our lives to the infiltration of the demonic hosts and potentially even possession. The bondage of demonic possession is largely unidentified now a days and results in inescapable bondage as a result.

is it? How powerful can it really be? If it is chosen by a person then it is not really superior to anyone and it will not be of much help to when someone is tempted and drawn away from abstinence. Only the Savior is capable of fulfilling that divine role without spot or blemish; He chooses us and gives us the grace to believe in Him. He is superior to everyone and thus is able to save us from our greatest temptations.

The Principle of Radical Amputation

The New Testament Gospel of Matthew 5 provides us with a look at what is necessary to eliminate the addictive substances and their harmful consequences in our lives. Matthew 5:27-30 records Jesus' words about abstaining from sin:

> "You have heard that it was said to those of old, 'You shall not commit adultery.' But I say to you that whoever looks at a woman to lust for her has already committed adultery with her in his heart. If your right eye causes you to sin, pluck it out and cast it from you; for it is more profitable for you that one of your members perish, than for your whole body to be cast into hell. And if your right hand causes you to sin, cut it off and cast it from you; for it is more profitable for you that one of your members perish, than for your whole body to be cast into hell."

The point that Christ is making here is that we have to be such lovers of God that we are willing to do whatever it takes to live a life that is pleasing to Him. It means that if we are serious about stopping our sins, we will go to such lengths that we may suffer in some painful measure to be rid of our sin. While He would not advocate the actual amputation of your arm, He is advocating the actual amputation of whatever causes us to stumble into sin.

This principle of radical amputation may extend to absolutely anything that hinders our walk with God. It may mean that we cease to associate with certain people, even people that we love dearly. They may be the closest or only friends that we have. But if they lure us into sin then we need new, healthy relationships. Many churches are good places to look for healthier relationships. Not all churches are good and not all people, even in good churches would afford healthy relationships. But it can be a good place to start looking if radical amputation is necessary.

This principle could be extended to include the places that tempt us. If going to a bar or a restaurant that serves liquor causes you to fall back into substance use or abuse, then cease attending there. You may even need to explain to a boss or family members that this is the real reason that you do not go out any more or cannot attend a function. If possible, share a word of your salvation testimony in the process and glorify God in it.

There may also be songs or things that serve as triggers to stir up your desires for substances, for escape, for the good ol days, and so on. You may need to change what radio station you listen to, or throw out something that has been dear to you while using. For some this may include coolers, or t-shirts worn whenever smoking illegal drugs, etc. If something causes you to turn back to your old habits it is best to be rid of it in keeping with this principle. Otherwise you sabotage your efforts to overcome your old habits permanently.

There is another principle that also applies here. It is the principle of expediency, which refers specifically to abstinence. The apostle Paul refers to it in two places in the book of 1 Corinthians. In 6:12 he says, "All things are lawful for me, but not all things are helpful. All things are lawful for me but I will not be enslaved by anything." And in 10:23 he says, "All things are lawful but not all things are helpful. All things are lawful but not all things build up."

We may well be within our legal rights to eat an entire package of cookies every day, but is it wise? Will it make us healthier? We may be living inside the law to watch eight hours of television every day or play videos for the entire evening but would it cause us to become enslaved to them? We may be neglecting other duties and obligations. It may be counter-productive. Discernment about the effects that result from such activities is necessary. If it draws us away from God then it is not a habit that should be permitted or cultivated.

There are Spiritual Consequences to Addiction

If a Christian insists upon continuing the sins of intoxication or addiction, then very real and serious spiritual consequences can be anticipated. The first such consequence is that of quenching the Holy Spirit's leading and illumination of the Word of

God. First Thessalonians 5:19 commands us not to quench the Spirit. If He is hindered in convicting us of our sins because we resist Him, then the promptings diminish over time. Just as it is pointless to tell a fool anything, so the Holy Spirit lets you take the consequences of hardening your heart against His loving promptings.

We stunt our growth in this manner and continue to sin. God's gifting to us the very indwelling of the Spirit of God is to help us conform to the image of His dear Son. Philippians 2:13 says, "it is God Who works in you both to will and to do for His good pleasure." Yet, simultaneously, we are to cooperate with Him by working out our own salvation with fear and trembling (Philippians 2:12). These two verses are paired together in this chapter. They compliment each other and depict the experience of every believer in living the Christian life, the balance of the mysterious workings of God in our Christian experience, and our efforts exerted to be like Him.

The second important spiritual consequence, which goes hand in hand with the first, is that of a seared conscience. What does this mean? The repetition of the hardening of the heart causes an insensitivity to moral principle and moral failure. We become less and less sensitive to the things of God. We do not hear the Holy Spirit any longer, we do not read the Bible, or if we do, we do not get much out of it. We do not pray, or we pray with great difficulty and it feels dead and dry. We fail to have love for God and for others. We can become liars and become deceptive as we slide back down a slope from righteous living in obedience to God into an ever-increasing state of unrighteous living in direct violation of God's commands, and eventually even outright rebellion against them.

So what do we do about this? Brokenness and repentance are the keys. God never rejects a genuinely humble and broken heart, especially when it is broken over our sin and brought to Him for repair and restoration. When we bring our brokenness to Him, and give it to Him, He gives us wholeness and restoration in our relationship to Him, and when possible, restoration and reconciliation with others.

Without the brokenness and repentance as a turning point in our lives, we will continue on the path of destruction. What we must do is determine to do right, to get an accountability partner, deny our selves, and thus our selfish desires, and walk in obedience to God's Word regardless of how trivial we think a commandment is. We must have a time of refreshment with the Lord. Fast and pray if that is what is necessary. Ask God for a soft heart that will love Him and obey Him no matter what. Because this is His desire for you, He will grant it to you. Keep at it.

A life of freedom awaits any person who will genuinely turn from sin and be obedient to God. This will be the only *real* living that you will ever do. Bondage to any sin, but especially something as multi-laterally destructive as drugs and alcohol, will never give anyone the "abundant life" that we all seek. Freedom comes only from Christ. Seek Him today.

Bitterness Vs. Forgiveness

One of the other extremely significant matters that must be addressed in dealing with PTSD is the matter of forgiveness against our "offenders." It is possible that others did us wrong and left us with PTSD in the wake. We need to forgive them. We need to abandon opportunities, or the longing for opportunities to take justice upon our enemies. The Emotion Code by Bradley Nelson is particularly helpful in this respect, freeing us to release those toxic emotions using his approach. Because many of these emotions are literally lodged in our physical bodies, especially in particular organs, they have a hold on us that is nothing short of bondage. Dr. Nelson's approach gives us an added boost to be victorious over these many challenging emotions. This has been such an effective tool in my life that an entire chapter of this book will be devoted to his method and material.

Vengeance belongs to God alone and hanging on to the desire to be like God and rule over our enemies for our own desired purposes is the sin of pride (Romans 12:17-21). Bitterness and unforgiveness enslave us to their sorrow, pain and the very impoverishment of our souls.

Robert D. Jones remarks with a hopeful truth when he says,

"The answer is found in Jesus. Jesus understands. He is with us. He comes to us in our mistreatment and remains with us to help us. As one who was sinned against severely, he understands mistreatment. He has been there. The Scriptures tell us that he came to save his own people but they did not receive him (John 1:11). 'He was despised and rejected by men, a man of sorrows, and familiar with suffering' (Isaiah 53:3). Jesus was sinned against severely: mocked, taunted, punched, spit upon, abandoned, and crucified. This is the Jesus - the mistreated one - who is with us and who is able to help us handle our resentment and overcome our bitterness."[42]

Bitterness

Bitterness is the accumulation of massive amounts of unforgiveness. It results in someone being intensely hostile or resentful of persons or events in which the person perceives s/he was wronged, or was actually wronged. There is a certain amount of truth to the fact that we are all done wrong, or have imagined that we have been done wrong, at various points. Some of these circumstances can be vicious or malicious in nature. Other times we have been the one to perpetrate such offenses against other people.

---

42 Jones, Robert. Freedom from Resentment. Stopping Hurts from Turning Bitter, p.6.

"There is nothing uglier than bitterness -- that inner anger lodged deep in the heart, sometimes known only to the bitter person (and his all-seeing God). Bitterness is *settled* anger, the kind that not merely reacts to someone's offense, but forms a more general and global animosity against the offender himself. Anger responds to an incident: 'I'm angry about *what you did*.' Bitterness goes deeper to form an attitude - a settled stance or posture - against the perpetrator: 'I'm bitter at *you*, because *you are* an evil person.' The incident becomes almost secondary."[43]

Regardless of the situation, sound theology requires an acknowledgement of the sovereignty of God in these events and a need to submit to the will of God. This makes things easier, though it often does not seem so at the onset or first suggestion of the thought. Romans 8:28 tells us that God can cause all things to work together for our good because of His great goodness with which He loves us. That is comforting.[44]

Hebrews 3:12-13 cautions us to beware of our own heart and its propensity to turn from God, even as believers. Even believers have hearts that can be hardened by the deceitfulness of sin.

---

43 Jones, Robert. *Freedom From Resentment. Stopping Hurts from Turning Bitter*, p. 5.

44 This book, birthed out of an entire life living in nothing but tribulation, is just such a situation. If God can turn around the nightmare that has been my life and use it to bring others to Christ or to help others to heal from PTSD, then He has had a great purpose in the suffering. Someone once said, "God is a great ecologist of our pain. He wastes nothing." Here's hoping so!

Our own bitterness destroys us. No one, including Christians, is immune from the dangers of a heart toxic with the sin of bitterness, deceived by its own "righteousness" in a situation, able to overlook its own heinous sin.

Forgiveness

So what is forgiveness? Is it the same as giving or receiving an apology? No, it is not. When someone apologizes, s/he is simply telling how s/he feels. Nothing has been asked of you. In apologies nothing is resolved because no one has accepted responsibility for wrong doing and no commitment of forgiveness is granted. This leaves the one offended often times, still offended. But, to ask someone for forgiveness for wrong doing is to ask that the matter be buried forever by both parties.

Forgiveness, then, is the releasing of our rights to get even, to take revenge, or to make someone suffer or pay for what was done to us or to our loved ones. These rights are not just released into thin air but rather are given to God to do with as He pleases, along with the surrender of the person(s) and even the results that we are bearing personally, or that our loved one is bearing (including the possibility of death). This releasing of our rights may have to be done repeatedly until we will no longer pick them up and hang onto them again.

You may cry out, "But that is not fair!" and you would be right because God is not fair. He is just. In the end He will see to it that what is righteous and just will be done in everyone's life, including our own. Justice may wait until the final judgment, but it will most certainly be done.

Sometimes it appears that the wicked are "getting away" with their sin. Psalm 73 explains that our view of life's inequities are settled once and for all by God's eternal destinations for sinners. Those who repent and believe in Jesus Christ will have eternal life and forgiveness of sins. Those who never believe will have eternal damnation. Often times, God chooses not to draw wicked people because if He gave them their just due here on earth they would repent and turn and believe. His character would be obligated to save them and He has not chosen them for salvation. So He lets them go on in their sins that He may punish them for all of eternity and be righteous in doing so. Other people find that they get negative consequences for everything they do and all sorts of evil keeps happening to them. God may very well be trying to get them to fall on their faces and ask for His divine intervention that He might save them and rescue them from their calamity. Yet they "kick against the goads" as the apostle Paul did (Acts 9:5). Whatever God is doing in people's lives, He *is* doing something!

This is where faith in the character of God comes into play. Learning from Scripture Who God really is and not just who we think He is, or not believing in whatever image of a god we have engraved in our own minds, but really knowing Who He *is* matters the most. Belief in the one true living God is necessary for this victory to be complete and for us to be whole again.

Forgiveness, to truly be effective in healing, must be modeled after God's forgiveness, and hence, must be studied and understood to be put into action. So what does God's forgiveness look like? Ephesians 4:32 says, "forgive one another just as God, for Christ's sake, has forgiven" us. When God forgives us, He does so through Christ.[45] In other words, when we receive forgiveness from God for the very first time it is based upon our faith in the person of Jesus Christ as the one and only unique Son of God, and in the salvific work He accomplished for us on the cross at Calvary.[46] When we ask God to apply His saving work to our sins (any and all), then He not only forgives us but He gives us eternal life and a new beginning. When we believe in Christ, He and the Holy Spirit come to live within us and begin immediately to transform us from who we are to who He had intended us to be: people that are like God's Son, Jesus the Christ.

Does it mean that God does not forgive us unless believe in Jesus as our Savior? Yes. Apart from saving faith, God is unable to forgive us because *payment for our sins must be made* and the only way that God has provided for payment is through the sacrificial death of Christ on the cross. Nothing that we could attempt to do would ever be sufficient. Isaiah 64:6 says that all of our "righteousness is like filthy rags."[47] Put simply, even our

---

45 Ephesians 1:7, Matthew 18:21-35

46 This work of Christ on the cross at Calvary is what is celebrated by Christians at Easter.

47 The Hebrew here is very explicit and offensive to consider: it is literally the filthy menstrual rags that women used for their periods. In the Middle East this would have given particular offense because the hot and

best efforts at being good or righteous before God are rejected as nothing but filthy undergarments. Only the perfect work of His sinless Son suffering in our place on the cross is sufficient to pay our sin debt so that we can be spared eternal punishment in Hell and be granted eternal life in heaven instead. He literally swaps His Son's righteousness for our sin, guilt and shame. We become blameless and holy before Him. This swapping of our sin for Christ's righteousness is the reason He can forgive our sins.

Forgiveness is not a feeling. It is a decision that becomes a *process* of letting go of hurts and offenses. Some hurts will need to be handled one by one while others will be let go in one massive chunk. For some people the moment that the decision is made to forgive, s/he is freed of the bondage. For others, the process of healing takes longer. And the longer unforgiveness is held onto, the harder it is to finally let go of it. The deeper it is established as a part of our being, the deeper the root of bitterness, the longer it takes to be free.

Taking the place of our unforgiveness is peace and/or love, a sense of calmness and freedom. This is worth far more than the longing only to see others hurt or made to pay for the suffering they have caused us. We lose all sense of justice when we seek revenge; our emotions, our will, and our desires make us poor determiners of what is just.

---

arid climate would have made them wreak quickly and badly, and they did not have much water in most places so cleaning at that time was a terrible chore.

Sometimes we withhold our forgiveness to punish the other(s). We feel a sense of empowerment by doing so, but that does not make us powerful nor does it hurt the others as much as it destroys us. Dr. Chuck Lynch says, "Withholding forgiveness until an offender understands or acknowledges the emotional pain they have inflicted is a subtle form of revenge. Why? Because it's hoping that the offender would hurt a little too, in order to understand. But this type of revenge robs you of your freedom and allows the offender to keep control over you."[48]

When God forgives us, He promises us that He will never remember those sins against us any longer! Isn't that amazing!? First John 1:9 tells us that "if we confess our sins, He is faithful and just to forgive us our sins and to cleanse us from all unrighteousness." That is total absolution of our sin debt! Isaiah 43:25 says, "I, even I, am He Who blots out your transgressions for My own sake; and I will not remember your sins." Here God states that He makes a point of actively not remembering our sins. As forgetting is a much more passive, even accidental occurrence, actively choosing to not remember is a decision to not think on them anymore. God no longer thinks on the sins that we have asked forgiveness for! He does not hold them against us any longer and never brings them up to us again, even if we do the same thing.

As much as God is willing to forgive the greatest sinner of the biggest debt, we have to ask Him for His forgiveness. We must

---

48 Dr. Chuck Lynch, *I Should Forgive, but. . . .* as quoted by Beth Moore in *Praying God's Word. Breaking Free From Spiritual Strongholds*, p. 226.

come by faith in Christ to the Father in heaven and ask Him to forgive us our sins and to cleanse us. We need to repent and believe in the person and finished work of Christ. We must *receive* the forgiveness of God i.e., receive Jesus Christ, or we live on in our guilt and shame, with our sinning haunting and dogging our every step, continuing to hold power over us, and able to destroy us and those around us.

But if we confess our need for forgiveness and our faith in Christ we are forgiven instantly! Romans 10.9&10 says that if we confess with our mouth and believe in our hearts that God raised Jesus from the dead then we will be saved. For with the heart one believes unto righteousness, and with the mouth confession is made unto salvation. Verse 13 says "for whoever calls on the name of the Lord shall be saved."

If you think that it is too easy, then why not try it?

Biblical Truths to Prevent Hurts from Becoming Bitterness

Bitterness reflects a failure to remember all that God has forgiven us. The enormity of our sin debt against God that He has freely forgiven when we believed in Christ as our Savior should never be easily set aside in our own memories. Consider what Christ said in Matthew 18:21-35. We are not to count the offenses of anyone but to forgive without limits. Failing to forgive brings severe consequences and bondage to the unforgiving.

Another item to note in this discussion is that Jesus unmistakably states that our heavenly Father's forgiveness of us depends somehow on our forgiving of others. We will make no progress in battling our bitternesses until we take to heart our Lord's warning: God withholds our forgiveness until we forgive others their trespasses against us (Matthew 6:12, 14-15; Mark 11:25). Forgiveness is suppose to be the mark of a Christian and therefore sets us apart from the lost world. If we are unforgiving, others will doubt our salvation and our testimony for Christ. To forgive is divine.

Another reason to overcome our bitterness is that we demonstrate the everlasting mercies of God to others and hence show the love of God to our neighbors. Loving our neighbors and our enemies is a command of Scripture; being a Christian means giving up the right to choose whom one will love. The fleshing out of the virtue of mercy in the life of a believer is another evidence of Christ at work in us. Micah 6:8 says, "He has showed you, O man, what is good. And what does the Lord require of you? To act justly, to love mercy and to walk humbly with your God." Luke 6:36 states, "Be merciful, just as your Father is merciful." Mercy is becoming to anyone, it becomes justice and the extension of mercy to others invites the mercy of God into our own lives. "Blessed are the merciful, for they shall be shown mercy" (Matthew 5:7).

Those of us who choose bitterness as a life-dominating response to the sins of others against us, or the tribulations of life, are also choosing the life-dominating sin of pride. The sin of bitterness sets us up in the place of God, the place of the judge. This self-exaltation to "godhood" is pure, unadulterated pride. James 4:12 warns us to leave judgment to God, as does Romans 12:19.

When we take the role of the judge we have considered the evidence against somebody, rendered our own "righteous" verdict, and determined the penalty for the other's guilt all in one fell swoop. While most people will acquiesce that this taking of vengeance is wrong, most likely few understand why it is. The pursuit of true justice and righteousness requires objectivity. This is a quality that only God understands or possesses. It is not that sin does not require a penalty, but rather that we are not the ones to render the verdict or the penalty. The decision belongs solely to God Himself. "It is mine to avenge; I will repay," says the Lord (Romans 12:19). It means that we have to trust God to be angry for us, and to handle our justice, in His own time, in whatever manner pleases Him.

Releasing our offenders to God and entrusting them to the Lord will free us from resentment that threatens to consume us, or at minimum, to sever our fellowship with God and others.

There is yet another perspective that requires consideration in preventing our hearts from becoming bitter with our offenders. Simply put, sin is enslaving. It cuts both ways: we are enslaved by our sin of bitterness, and our offenders are enslaved by the sins that blind them and deceive them. Christ said, "Everyone who sins is a slave to sin" (John 8:34). Second Peter 2:19 says, "a man is a slave to whatever has mastered him," and we are told in Proverbs 5:22 that "the evil deeds of a wicked man ensnare him; the cords of his sin hold him fast." Our sins, and those of our neighbors, are the same and have the same result: slavery to those sins.

While no excuses can be offered for people's sin choices, we must endeavor to look upon our offenders as God sees them. If we can learn not to take the persons' sins too personally, we may find it easier to muster compassion for those who, like us, are enslaved by sin. Ultimately, the person's sins were against God much more so than against us. God still commended His love towards us while we were sinners, and His enemies, which evidences His desire for us to do the same.

If we will humble ourselves and pull the beam out of our own eye before taking specks from someone else's, we will see that we are likely guilty of the same sins as others. Someone once said, "All of us are like the rest of us." We are all fallible. We all sin and fall short of the glory of God (Romans 3:23). We each need the same mercy and forgiveness of God, and others, just as the next sinner. We are not better than others in terms of sinlessness; our bitterness permits us to be naïve about our own moral superiority and remain self-deceived regarding our vulnerability to commit the same sins as our offenders. The humility to see this and believe it in our hearts will help us develop the virtues of compassion and mercy for the worst offenders. No one is better than another. We can all say, "But for the grace of God, there go I."

Forgiveness After Salvation

If we have indeed accepted Christ, and are therefore forgiven, then why would we be consistently asking others for forgiveness after this? When the sins that we commit after we have been saved interrupt our fellowship with God, then our communication has to be reestablished through repentance and the seeking of forgiveness for those specific sins only. We must also humbly accept and receive that forgiveness from Him. In this manner our fellowship and communication are reestablished and our prayers are no longer hindered between us and God. It is reconciliation with God and thereby the restoration of the relationship.[49]

Forgiving & Forgetting

While God actively chooses to not remember our sins against us any longer, we are not so amnesia-gifted. This makes the process for Christians three-fold. First, we choose not to dwell on the others' sins against us in our own mind. This necessitates that when they come to mind we deliberately choose to set them aside. Scripture calls it "taking our thoughts captive" and commanding them to become obedient to us (2 Corinthians 10.5). Given the intrusive nature of some of these thoughts, this can be very challenging. There are certain lines of thought that our minds are bent on; paths that must be severed and new thoughts substituted, such as Scripture passages that we have memorized or songs of praise and worship. But persistence pays off, *so persist in your efforts.*

The second thing in forgiving and forgetting is that we make the decision not to bring up the person's sins against us to anyone else, even as a prayer request. If we are letting it go in sincere forgiveness, then we must cease any discussion of the matter.

---

49 An entire chapter of this book is devoted to the issues of reconciliation.

Remember, we cannot discuss it with others and not be thinking on it in our own mind.

Thirdly, we must decide not to bring it up to that person again, including the next time the person does the same thing. This is very difficult. Genuine repentance may only last moments before the same thing is done again. Learning to overcome a sin habit takes time. Someone who decides to stop a sin may find that s/he goes from committing that sin 100 times per day to 50 times per day to eventually seven times per week to once a month to once every nine months and so on. As we get better at replacing our sin habits with righteous ones, our frequency of sinning is usually reduced. This should be encouraging to both those sinning and to those being sinned against. It is also encouraging to know that when we choose not to think on these things *we do actually forget them!* But remember, forgiving is the only way to get here.

The reason this is so is because forgiveness is not an end in and of itself but rather is to serve as the means to an end. The "end" is restoration between us and an offended party. If handled properly, then the relationship will be even better after the altercation than it was before. We will have greater love for the other person, regardless of which side of the issue we are on. When we are forgiven by God, He doesn't just wash His hands of us and go on as if we no longer exist to Him. Instead, He establishes a new and vital relationship with us that continues to grow and blossom, making us better people, more like His Son, Jesus. This is precisely what we are suppose to do as well.

What About Forgiving Ourselves?

Because so very much has been said in the self-esteem movement about loving oneself and forgiving yourself it needs to be addressed.

First of all, Scripture is the rule of faith and practice and *absolutely nowhere does the Word of God command us to either love ourselves nor forgive ourselves!* So where did this lie come from? The entire self-esteem movement, which is given wholly to the preoccupation of oneself with one's self, is desperately heretical.[50] We already love ourselves more than we will ever love our neighbors and *that* is why Christ uses it the standard of how we ought to love others: if we would be as concerned for others as we are for ourselves, the world would be a better place! Not because He is directing us to love ourselves. This is foolishness, to say the very least. If we loved others the way we focus on ourselves, then we would have no room to worry about our own selfish self interests.

The same needs to be said about forgiving one's self. We all have made mistakes that we regret and repent of deeply. We all sin. What we need is the forgiveness of God - and to accept forgiveness from Him is key to having peace about those sins. When we receive God's forgiveness, we need never ask for it again; we never have to bring up that matter to Him again and ask Him to forgive us for that instance again. If we should commit the same sin again God does not bring up the other instance(s) that

---

50 An excellent and thorough source on this subject matter is Jay Adam's book The Biblical View of Self-esteem, Self-love , Self-image , Harvest House Publishers, 1986.

we have asked forgiveness for already. It is important to realize this because this is a model of how we are suppose to forgive, including when people perpetuate the same sin habit against us for the "umpteenth time".

What we really need to do is receive God's forgiveness and accept that there are consequences that the sovereignty of God has control over and He will direct these consequences according to His divine purposes in using them for His honor and glory, and our good. Submitting to this Lordship of Christ will help us accept and deal with the negative consequences that remain after repentance, confession and the receiving of His forgiveness.

We are unable to forgive our own sins because we are unable to atone for our own sins. Christ's atonement alone is satisfactory. Sin is failure to obey God on some point, to miss His mark of perfection and holiness. We either do something that we are forbidden to do or we fail to do what we are commanded to do. He who knows what is good and does not do it, to him it is sin. But if we supposedly "fail to forgive ourselves" we have not sinned.[51]

The reason people try to forgive themselves is to overcome the feeling that something more needs to be done. People find themselves overcome with guilt and want to resolve that guilt. But they are still guilty. They are unchanged by simply desiring to be guilt-free. They need something further: forgiveness of sin. But since we don't have the power to forgive ourselves,

---

51 I challenge anyone to demonstrate from any clear command of Scripture, or from a clear theological argument supported from Scripture, that God commands us to forgive ourselves.

we are left hanging, wondering what is wrong and what should be done to resolve our guilt.

To overcome the faults that led to the need to forgive oneself, one needs fundamental changes on the inside, changes that are so radical that only the power of the living God within you can wrought them. This requires saving faith and knowledge of the Word of God to grow inside of us and empower us to overcome our faults and heal our guilt. The truth will set you free. Once again, it is faith in Christ that will heal our guilt and provide us forgiveness for our sins - the ultimate healing for a guilty sinner.

Reconciliation

I have opted to make this a separate chapter from the chapter on forgiveness. My reason for this is that it is not always applicable to an individual's trauma. There are many events which can occur that are traumatizing and do not involve a personal sin against the recipient, (i.e., natural disasters, the collapse of the I-35 bridge in Minneapolis, and so forth).

We must consider that we might be on both sides of this issue. We may be offended by someone's sin and we may also have offended others. Perhaps any situation may be a combination of these elements. However, we remain responsible for our own sins and our part in aggravating a matter or in precipitating one. Victims of trauma often perpetuate trauma in their own lives, and the lives of others, by repeating them in ignorance against others. Child abuse and alcoholism are two such sins.

It is my hope to help people gain a deeper measure of understanding about what to do and where to start in trying to make things right that have been done wrong. Accepting God's forgiveness through salvation in Christ is the first step. But all of us have done others wrong, and sometimes egregiously so, and we need to do our part to make it right. People may have died, be unreachable, unwilling to hear, unwilling to forgive and a myriad of other options. However, it is the responsibility of the one who has sinned to go to the one sinned against and ask for forgiveness.

Whenever we sin against others, we sin against God, too. Consequently, there can never be a time that we sinned against someone else and don't need to ask God's forgiveness as well. In fact, they are bound together. We cannot seek someone else's forgiveness and fail to seek God's forgiveness and still believe that we have right fellowship restored with God. Neither can we restore relationship with God and remain unreconciled to our brother against whom we have sinned. One necessitates the other.

Not all sins are made manifest outwardly. Some of them are what are termed heart sins. These sins are known by the sinner and by God alone. The one, or ones, to whom it is directed is unaware of it. If these sins are dealt with prior to manifesting themselves outwardly, then it is where they should remain. Reconciliation with God alone at that point is sufficient. It would be unwise, and often times hurtful, to mention them to the other person at all, and could even provoke others to sin in return.

For those sins that we have outwardly committed against others, Scripture has some things to say. Matthew 5:23-26 says,

> "So then, if you are offering your gift at the altar, and there remember that your brother has something against you, leave

your gift right there in front of the altar, and go first and be reconciled to your brother; then come and offer your gift. Quickly come to terms with your legal opponent, while you are with him on the way; otherwise your opponent may hand you over to the judge, and the judge to his officer, and you will be thrown into prison. Let me assure you that you surely will not get out of there until you have paid the last cent."

Both the phrases "go first" and "quickly come to terms" stress the urgency of the need to be reconciled. To be on good terms with God, we must be on right terms with others, as much as it is up to us (Romans 12:18 and Hebrews 12:14).

Several things should be noted about the attempts made at reconciliation. First, it is best if you go to the person first and not wait until you are found out or cornered. This confession and seeking of forgiveness is a sign of genuine repentance. Discretion about what should be said and how it should be phrased needs to be exercised in every situation or it could become exacerbated. For precisely this reason, it is critical that we not go justifying ourselves and blaming anyone else. We must take full responsibility for what we have done and humbly ask for forgiveness. We must not corner or nail someone else for his or her part in provoking us and so forth. Simply stick to the part for which you, yourself, are responsible or the situation may deteriorate into yet another offense.

If the person(s) to whom you went is unwilling to hear you or forgive you then you have done what you can. Simply remain quiet, difficult as that may seem. It is possible that it will take time for the person to come around and become willing to hear and forgive. This depends upon the person and the nature and severity of the offense. Be patient, be gentle and be kind. Healing takes time.

When Reconciliation is not Possible

I could not begin to enumerate the reasons that reconciliation is not always possible. But death is one of them. Sometimes we cannot locate them to attempt making amends. Other times they will not hear us even if we have finally found them and gone to them. Others may not acknowledge the truth and will not repent. Reconciliation, conditioned upon repentance that includes acknowledging the truth of our sins against people, is never going to happen if someone refuses to speak the truth about what was done, or said, that caused the injury.

There are times that this healing process should be pursued between parties and it will not lead to having a relationship with that person. One notable and public example is that of Tyler Perry who posted on the internet the story of his father who beat him mercilessly for no explicable reason. After reading his story, I am certain within myself that Mr. Perry's father is demonically possessed, same as my own mother. That alone explains the beating.[52] Mr. Perry has discontinued his relationship with

---

52 This really struck a cord with me, as I have found that my own biological mother suffers from the same problem of demonic possession and the same violent rages resulting in the same senseless beatings that were nothing short of cruelty.

his father, the same thing that I had to do with my own mother, because there is no hope for these relationships until Christ enters their hearts and Satan is no longer given the latitude that he has in their lives, and thus in their relationships; apart from redemption and demonic deliverance, these people and these relationships will remain unchanged. He states that he forgives his father but will not have a relationship with him. I applaud both of his decisions; they are both right.

When there are such cases of domestic violence, cruelty, sexual abuse and so forth, it is not only wise to discontinue a relationship with the other party, but it is morally necessary. It is in our own best interests to choose wise and mutually beneficial relationships, but we continue to aid and abet people in the committing of sin by tolerating it or associating with it. The perpetrators of these abuses will not grow without the consequences of the sins they have chosen. Prosecution is sometimes necessary and is not an indication that we are unforgiving or unwilling to forgive. Rather it is in the best interest of the perpetrator to face the righteous consequences for his or her actions. According to Hebrews 12:3-11, it is a demonstration of the highest form of biblical love.

The author here acquiesces that each situation is individual and what course of action a person takes after the biblical steps have been completed is dependent upon the parties involved and the circumstances. If you have obeyed God to the best of your ability and it is still unresolved then move on. Not every situation, though responded to biblically will result in the best case scenario. As disappointing as this is, it is reality. Be prepared.

The Emotion Code:
Emotional Release of Toxic Emotions

I have been introduced to an extraordinary book that has truly changed my life. In June of 2010 I learned of Dr. Bradley Nelson and his method for releasing toxic emotions that are caught inside of us and need to be purged in order for us to have a fuller, freer life. The first effort that we made at this was, for me, just an experiment. But, given what I had lived, if it could work, then the good that could result was too much to pass up. Thank the Lord that I tried it! It was fabulous! I have learned from her, over the course of many sessions, enough to continue on my own. I also purchased his book, *The Emotion Code*[53] and read it. It was eye-opening, to say the least.[54]

Now I realize that to a skeptic, most especially those in conservative Christianity, this will very possibly sound like hog wash.

---

53 ISBN: 978-0-9795537-0-7

54 Please note that on the last two pages of his book, Dr. Nelson offers the book for free to any soldier with PTSD. What they get is an offer of an eBook of the material. TheEmotionCode.com/SaveaSoldier

It is not; it really works. Because of the amazing results that I have obtained by following his methods, I absolutely could not publish this book without sharing the vast degree of hope that is entailed in emotional freedom.

I have been using the emotion code since June, 2010 to process out toxic thoughts & emotions. The relief that I have experienced with regard to my PTSD alone makes this a worthwhile quest to share. I now awaken without violent and intrusive thoughts, which have been such a standard in my life; all of my PTSD symptoms have been reduced by probably more than 90%! I *have* to share this information!

In my personal pursuits to overcome PTSD in my life I have found that only salvation, and the indwelling of the Spirit of God, is superior to this method of actively pursuing victory over the past and the bondage that it creates within. While I will share some of the information in this book, nothing, it should be noted, can really replace the value of reading the totality of what the book says. In other words, read *The Emotion Code* yourself.

You should also contact www.healerslibrary.com to find someone in your area that would be willing to assist you in getting started with this approach to emotional detoxification. Apart from releasing emotions that literally get trapped inside of our bodies, we will never totally be free of their bondage. Things you and I have long since forgotten about are still there and still affecting us negatively. Anything that you can readily recall as traumatic and emotional is still lodged, in some capacity, inside your being. These emotions can be intense and destructive. They are a poison to our lives, our relationships and our souls. Being rid of them is incredibly important.

All of us have experienced negative emotions, whether ours or someone else's. Sometimes their emotions transfer to us. These are referred to as inherited emotions. If we clear it for ourselves, it will clear for someone else, too. What a cause for rejoicing!

These negative emotions can continue to create problems for us years after we originally felt them, in subtle and damaging ways. This is about finding them and releasing them forever. And why not let them go? They can cause us both physical and emotional problems. Once they are gone, our bodies can also begin to heal and function properly again. The freedom, the lightness, is like nothing else! I am living proof that when you let enough of these things go that you can live a healthier and happier life!

Personal Testimonial of Results from Using the Emotion Code

I would like to briefly share some of the benefits that I have experienced from releasing trapped emotions and what I call "scripts" utilizing a magnet.

My thyroid gland had completely failed and I was on total thyroid support medication. After pinpointing approximately 19 trapped emotions and scripts trapped in the thyroid I ceased taking the medication and tests now confirm that it is fully operational on its own! I have also released everything that I have been able to find related to my service-connected asthma and I am off of the asthma medications, too! I have likewise discovered that I have extensive plaque build up on my main artery. It is mostly due to trapped emotions and is already shrinking substantially since releasing those items.

Since releasing so much stuff I find that my kidneys are functioning so much better. After questioning my body it confirmed that in fact many trapped emotions that have been released were trapped in my kidneys, impairing their efficiency. Now they are operating at a level I have not seen in 20 years!

These are not all of the things that are healthier in my own body but I am confident that it will encourage people to address their own health problems from this perspective and thereby improve not just their emotional health but their physical health, too.

What is a Trapped Emotion?

All of us can and do experience negative emotions at times, sometimes in extremes, as in PTSD. The influence of these events can stay with us in the form of trapped emotions. For some reason, some emotional experiences do not process completely. The emotional energies somehow become "trapped" within our physical bodies. Our emotional baggage becomes more literal than we thought!

186

These trapped emotions actually consist of well-defined energies that have a shape and form.[55] Although they are not visible, they are very real. It is the particular arrangement of these energies, and their specific rates of vibration, that determine how they will appear to us. We can feel these energies in the form of emotions, and if the negative emotional energies become trapped within us they can affect us in very adverse ways.

Have you ever felt like you struggle under the burden of something that you cannot identify? Many of us unconsciously sabotage our lives in destructive ways. Perhaps your efforts at having lasting relationships never seem to work out (common to those with PTSD). You may wish events in your past had never occurred but you feel powerless to overcome their impact on you. Your may feel like your present is being held hostage by your past in ways you cannot define. Many people struggle with these things. What we often do not realize is that we are being controlled in subtle and unconscious ways by trapped emotions from our past that are sabotaging our efforts to live our lives now.

These trapped emotions can cause us to make the wrong assumptions, overreact to innocent remarks, misinterpret behavior and short-circuit our relationships. These same emotions are making everything in your life toxic because they have made *you* toxic, and they can also create other toxic emotions such as depression, anxiety and other emotions that you seem to be unable to shake. These unhealed wounds, when released, can be a

---

55 Nelson, Bradley, The Emotion Code, p. 5.

burden lifted and the person can literally feel lighter physically. These changes will alter the way that you feel and behave, the choices that you make and the results that you get in virtually every area of your life.

When I finally took down the entirety of my heart wall (discussed later) the entire world around me became a friendlier place. People smiled at me more often, started casual conversations out of the blue more often and more easily, and I participated in them more readily, with less fear than before. The world around me sensed that I had changed, and most of these people were people that I did not even know.

The releasing of these emotions allows the person to become who he or she was really intended by God to become; the very best *you*. Not only do you get substantially more enjoyment out of life, but others enjoy your company a great deal more, and you enjoy theirs more. The whole of a relationship can be detoxified if you, yourself, become less encumbered by the negativity you are hauling around. This is true of anyone, but it is especially true of those with PTSD.

Retrieving the Data through Muscle Testing

I had already been exposed to this muscle testing, otherwise known as kinesiology, from the herbal store clerk who tested me for appropriateness of individual supplements, etc. using this approach. So I already knew that it worked. If you are not familiar with it please bear in mind that it is used every day by those familiar with it and they have had great success. In fact, this is how my toxic emotions were identified and released them.

Robert Frost says,

> "Your subconscious is also aware of exactly what your body needs in order to get well. But how can you get to this information?"
> "I began asking myself that same question when I was in chiropractic school. I learned that the brain is essentially a computer, the most powerful computer in the known universe. This made me wonder if healers would ever be able to tap into the immense power of the brain, to find critical information about what was wrong with their patients."
> "During my years of practice, I learned that it is actually possible to retrieve information from the subconscious, using a form of kinesiology, or muscle testing. First developed by Dr. George Goodheart in the 1960's as a way to correct structural imbalance in the skeleton, muscle testing is now widely accepted. While many physicians worldwide use muscle testing procedures to correct spinal misalignments and other imbalances, the fact that muscle testing can be used to get information directly from the subconscious mind is less recognized."[56]

When using this approach, it is key to note that your body is drawn toward positive things or thoughts and repelled by

---

56 Robert Frost, *Applied Kinesiology: A Training Manual and Reference Book of Basic Principles and Practice*, p. 4.

negative things or ideas. This is critical in using the simplest method, the Sway Test. So far it is the only one that I have been able to master; I have not mastered any of the other methods listed in Dr. Nelson's book.

To try the Sway Test, assume a standing position and make sure you are comfortable. The room should be quiet and free of distractions. It is best if you learn this when you are alone or with someone else who is learning it, too.

Stand with your feet shoulder width apart so that you are comfortably balanced. Stand still, with your hands by your sides. Let go of all your worries and relax your body completely. Close your eyes if you are comfortable doing so. This will require that you allow your body to be in control of itself and not you. For some people this is very challenging, even frightening. This is why you may wish to be alone to begin with.

When you make a positive, true or congruent statement, your body should begin to sway noticeably forward, usually in less than 10 seconds. When you make an incongruent or untrue statement you will notice your body sways backwards in the same period of time.

You can start by testing this with your name. "My name is _____". If you give your real name your body will sway forward. If you give a false name your body will sway backwards. You can use anything, birthdates, relationships (I am married) and so forth. When you have the feel of this you can then begin asking questions that you do not consciously know the answer to, for example, "Do I have an organ imbalance from a trapped emotion?" and similar questions.

You can ask these questions silently to yourself or you can ask them out loud. The results should be the same. But keep your mind clear and focused; if your thoughts constantly wander, then your subconscious will have difficulty determining what to respond to. Have patience with yourself! The more you practice, the more you will succeed at it.

Trapped Emotions & the Cause of Illness

Thousands of years ago physicians realized that people who lived their lives dominated by certain emotions would eventually manifest corresponding physical illnesses. For example, people who lived their lives ruled by anger seemed to have liver and gall bladder troubles. Those living with grief would often times suffer from lung or colon trouble. Fearful people seemed to have kidney and bladder problems.

Dr. Nelson's chart in the book identifies these emotions and their corresponding physically affected areas. It surely seems to hold up true in my own experience. As my emotional healing progresses so does my physical recovery from other things that have challenged me for years, sometimes as long as I can even remember.

Our entire bodies are intelligent, not just our brains. Your organs are separate intelligences within your body that perform certain functions and produce specific emotions or feelings. People are usually surprised to learn that the various organs in our bodies produce the emotions that we feel, but there are strong correlations to this principle in life and they are very distinct.

If you have an organ that is diseased, over stimulated, or imbalanced in some way, the emotions related to that organ will often be heightened. Our trapped emotions are found to have emanated from a particular organ, regardless of where it chooses ultimately to lodge inside the body.

The Reason That Emotional Release Works

Our thoughts have great power. We have the power to use the energy of our thoughts, directed intentionally, to impact other people, even if they are somewhere else in the world. This especially works with inherited psychic trauma[57] or inherited trapped emotions. These trapped toxicities originated with someone else and somehow became transferred to us and trapped within our bodies. We can clear these out for ourselves, and in the process they can be cleared for the other person, too.[58]

---

57 A psychic trauma is two or more emotions that are trapped together and need to be released together. I have found in my own experience that there can be many and all of them need to be identified and released. The question should be posed to the participant, "How many trapped emotions are there in this psychic trauma?"

58 I have actually found a despair anchor and a psychic trauma (two or more emotions that were trapped together regarding the same thing) that I had inherited from a former friend, which she had inherited from someone

When I direct my positive thought energy at other people with the intention of doing them good, as in assisting them in releasing negative emotions, my positive thought energy helps them to be free of their baggage. Believe it or not, this really works and is the basis for this method. It also works to clear things on myself, as I have been doing for months.

It should also be noted here that if you have trapped emotions you will attract more of that emotion into your own life. You will also tend to feel that emotion more readily and more often than you otherwise would. For example, if you are in a situation that you could become angry you likely will become angry because in a literal way, a part of you is already angry. Our trapped emotions cause us to resonate with that negative energy rather than go against the energy current. In reality, we get used to having that emotion as a part of us, and we set ourselves up for repeated failure with respect to that negative energy or negative emotion.

The Physical Effects of Trapped Emotions

Tissues that are constantly distorted by negative emotions will eventually suffer from those effects. Dr. Nelson mentioned that

---

else! Instead of passing the magnet 10 times to rid both myself and the one I inherited it from, I had to pass the magnet 15 times (I learned this number by applied kinesiology) to clear it for all three of us. I have never met the woman that had originated them but in a week it should have cleared for all of us. It was so powerful that, years later, it is still passing to other people who are totally unaware of it. Now both of them will be free of it, too!

every cancer patient that he has ever treated has been found to have trapped emotions embedded in the malignant tissues.[59] In other words, those trapped emotions caused the cancer and when released the cancer is overcome by the body. We have long understood that there is a link between our emotional and spiritual health and our bodies but this adds some illumination to that discussion!

If the essential cause of your illness is not dealt with, then your illness will not heal, or will recur. Most of us never realized that there is an emotional component to our illness and hence have never dealt with that aspect. But by facing these issues, we can facilitate our body's ability to heal itself. It will be freer to fight off disease or whatever ails us.

How Our Thoughts Affect Others

There is a spiritual side to every human being and our thoughts are a part of us as much as our spirit is. They affect one another in some circular or synergistic manner. Likewise, our spirit and our thoughts both can have a profound impact on those around us, emanating from our bodies without limits.

Our thoughts not only affect the energy field of others but of ourselves, too. If we switch our positive thoughts to a negative line of thinking it drastically affects the vibrational energy from positive to negative. Inevitably, we will have an obvious weakening of the body. Our subconscious is aware of these negative

---

59 www.TheEmotionCode.com

thoughts and how they harm us whether they originated with us or not.

Intention is another form of thought energy. One could refer to it as directed thought energy. While it is possible to release trapped emotions using the power of your intention alone, i.e., the desire to forgive others' their sins against us, it is magnified by the use of magnets. The magnets literally magnify your thought-energy and intention beyond your normal capacity. This makes it possible for anyone to release trapped emotions. No real experience is necessary. And personally, I have found that the most difficult part of forgiveness is the pain that we have experienced emotionally. If that pain can be overcome then forgiveness is easy.

While there are magnets designed just for healing the body any magnet will usually work. They magnify your intention and then carry that into the energy field of your body, though the positive intention is probably the most important aspect of the equation. Magnets simply intensify the thoughts that you have and their effect on you or others.

So where do you pass the magnet? Over the Governing Meridian. Where's that, you ask? It runs the length of your central nervous system, the brain and the spinal column. To affect change in this energy field of neurological activity we overcome it with another form of energy, namely magnets.[60]

---

60 There are specific biomagnets available from Nikken, a Japanese company. Personally I bought some magnets from the craft store and put them

While holding the intention in your mind to release the trapped emotion that you have found, pass the magnet over the Governing Meridian. Your magnified intention to release the trapped emotion enters into the Governing Meridian and the thought-energy flows quickly into all the other meridians of your body and hence the whole of your body. This influx of positive energy has the effect of releasing the trapped emotions from the areas of the body that they are literally stored in. The energy that we infuse into the meridians with the magnets literally overpowers the vibrational frequency of the trapped emotions and cancels them out. Basically, you create an opposing energy that overwhelms the trapped emotion's frequency setting it free from your body.[61]

Energy itself can obey or cooperate with our intentions. The universe seems to develop a resonance with us that reinforces our beliefs, whether they are positive or negative. If we believe that we cannot do this or that, then we will not be able to. But if we believe that we can then the universe will agree with us and we will succeed.

This fact lends itself in mighty ways to the success of emotional release. My success the first time that I tried releasing emotions has become a very positive thought energy within me that lends

---

altogether. It has been working just fine for me. It is not necessary to spend a great deal of money on a magnet to achieve these results.

61 It should be duly noted that magnets are considered very safe for most people. Some exceptions exist and a physician may need to be consulted. If you are pregnant, have implanted pain devices, insulin pumps cochlear implants or pacemakers you should consult a physician before attempting emotional release with the addition of magnets to your positive intentions.

itself favorably every time that I do another clearing. But those that decide to be negative about it find that it does not work for them; their skepticism is confirmed. To be a healer using the emotion code you cannot entertain doubts. Fill your heart with love and gratitude to God for the gift of freedom that it will give you and the positive results that it will have in your life and that of others *and it will work*!

I personally developed amnesia about what had processed out because it was so thoroughly gone. There is not a recorded instance that I am aware of that the trapped emotions ever returned or resurfaced. However, you may have many more items trapped regarding an event or person that must be released in order for that matter to totally cease to have a grip on you. All of them will need to be released for complete freedom to ensue.

Getting Answers from the Inner Mind Via Muscle Testing[62]

The most widely used and accepted method of assessing the internal computer system of the body is known variously as muscle testing, kinesthetic testing or applied kinesiology. It can tell us about the overall health and balance of our bodies in a direct manner. When we believe we have pinpointed the information we are looking for, then we can double-check our answers for correctness using the same approach. Muscle testing provides a

---

62 Much of this section will be quoted directly from the ebook *The Emotion Code* available at www.healerslibrary.com.

real window into what is going on in the body's mind. Using muscle testing, we can literally gain access to our body's internal computer system and find out where the imbalances are. It is very effective and very quick. Once you learn what questions to ask, a skill that is developed over time, it is tremendous at getting to the root of the problem.

We can also use this on others to help them. When our energy fields connect with each other, we are able to project our positive thought energy into their energy field and release their toxic emotions, too. We can also use a proxy to get this done, in other words, a third person.

The Basic Arm Test (to another person)

First of all, ask the person you wish to test if they have pain in either shoulder. If they do, don't use that arm as it may aggravate their condition. If they have trouble in both shoulders or if they are too young, too weak, or too ill to be tested then you need another person, a surrogate, to test them.

1. Ask the subject you wish to test to stand up and hold one arm out directly in front of them, horizontal to the floor. They should not make a tight fist, but let their hand remain relaxed.

2. Place the first two fingers of one hand lightly on their arm, just above the wrist.

3. Place your free hand on their opposite shoulder to support them.

4. Tell the subject "I'm going to have you make a statement, and then I'm going to press down on your arm. I want you to resist me by holding your arm right where it is; try to prevent me from pushing your arm down."

5. Have the subject state his or her name. "My name is _____."

6. Perform the muscle test by smoothly and steadily increasing the pressure downward on the subject's arm, going from no pressure to a fairly firm pressure within about 3 seconds.

7. The shoulder joint should stay "locked" against your firm downward pressure, and should not give way.

If the statement the person made is true the arm should stay locked. If it is false it will give way. Test both true and false statements before seeking the information that you do not know for certain. Everyone is different and it is essential to establish a baseline of resistance with each person or you will not know if a statement is congruent or incongruent.

Anyone's arm could easily become fatigued if you use too much force; muscle testing does not require the use of brute force. Always use the minimum force necessary to perceive whether the arm is staying locked or not. If pain or discomfort occur either the duration of testing has been too long or too much force is being used.

Remember that the person to be tested must consent to be tested. Do not violate the person's right to decline testing. This is grossly unethical. If the person is cynical or skeptical the testing will not be as productive or simple to do. Do not waste time on people who do not want your help. If they are not open to this approach then do not argue the point with them. Respect the decision.

There are other types of testing elucidated in *The Emotion Code* but these basics can get anyone started. There are also cautions and warnings included in the book that are wise to heed. One caution in particular is that those of us using it cannot make a diagnosis unless we are also medically licensed. You may discern enough to recommend they see a doctor for diagnosis or treatment but unless you are professionally qualified do not make an official diagnosis.

Our "inner mind" that is being tested here is the subconscious mind. It taps into the spiritual realm and I have personally tested myself as to whether spiritual information can be obtained using applied kinesiology, too, and the answer was affirmative, or at least to some extent. When I have violent and intrusive thoughts I will quiz myself on occasion to find out if they are stemming from PTSD or just my sin nature. Usually they are a result of PTSD and testing has indicated that they will go away when I have fully cleared myself. Sure enough, as I have been doing this for months now, some of which have been intensively directed at PTSD-causing problems, my thoughts have calmed markedly. This gives me great hope that my healing is a joint effort between me and my Savior! God is at work and He is healing me!

Releasing Trapped Emotions

The first and perhaps the most important matter is that the subject has to grant permission for this process to occur. Never perform this on someone without permission. Be sure that children have their legal parent or guardian consulted prior to treatment.

Secondly, because every person is unique, we have to establish a baseline for each subject. If for some reason the subject is unable to be tested directly then establish a proxy's baseline.

One reason that you try to establish a baseline is to determine if the person is testable at this time. If the person remains strong or weak, regardless of what question you ask (either true or false) then the person is not testable. If someone is untestable it is possible that he or she is dehydrated. Merely drinking some water will solve the issue. Or it is possible that there is a misalignment in the spine and the nerves are not functioning properly. If this has been the case for a long time then proper chiropractic care will be necessary to have a testable subject. Again, using a proxy may be the best option.

The third step is to determine if a trapped emotion exists. It is virtually impossible, upon first testing people, for an individual subject to have no trapped emotions. But whether it is the cause of any particular problem that you are trying to resolve is another matter. Learning to ask the right questions is key to the process.

If you instruct the person to make the statement, "I have a trapped emotion that can be released now" and the person tests strong for this statement then proceed to number four. If, however, the body says there is no trapped emotion that can be released at this time then several things could be true. First, though unlikely, the person really does not have any trapped emotions. Second, the subject's subconscious mind does not want to release any trapped emotions at this time. This could conceivably change over time upon subsequent testing. And the third possibility is that the person has what is called a heart wall, discussed further on.

The fourth step in the process of releasing trapped emotions is to use the chart provided in The Emotion Code. There are 60 emotions divided into columns and rows. Begin by asking is it column A or B? Odd or even row and then narrow it down from there.

I personally always ask myself at what age the item I am trying to clear occurred. It helps me understand myself more and I have tracked these things now for months. You can also ask where in the body it was lodged, or if it contributed to anything else that is a problem.

Proceed to pass the magnet at least three times over the head and down the spinal column. If the emotion or trauma is inherited, it will require 10 passes. And, as I just recently discovered, if you have inherited something that someone else inherited then it will take 15 passes of the magnet! But when inherited emotions or traumas are cleared, they are also cleared for the other person, no matter where he or she is in the world!

Once you have found the emotion to be cleared on the chart, it is necessary to bring that to the conscious awareness of the subject. The emotion must find expression in order to be released. This validates the emotion and brings a degree of closure to the situation that caused it. If the trapped emotion is given its "voice," it will be able to leave. If that does not happen, then the emotion will continue to make its presence known by creating physical pain and/or emotional dysfunction.

If the emotion will not release, then you may have to ask, "Is there more that we need to know to release it?" If the answer is yes, then dig deeper. If the answer is negative, then simply release it.

Be certain that you inquire as to whether or not the emotion was released. If the answer is no then try passing the magnet three times again and ask again if it was released. If the answer is still no then you may need to find out whose emotion it was or dig deeper. It is possible that you may need to specify in your question, "Is this emotion inherited?" or "Is this emotion hidden?"

It is also possible that it is being blocked by something else that has to be released first. This has happened to me frequently. As many as seven items had to be cleared before that single item was ready to release. You can use the same flow chart method in asking for that information.

This method of releasing trapped emotions can also be used to hone in on certain specific issues, whether they be events or people. This may become very important, especially for victims of PTSD. I myself have used this method to target specifically things that are related to my having PTSD. Some very interesting things continue to surface. Others will need to be able to target things specifically and narrow in the healing efforts directly to those areas that most deeply affect them.

Column A

1. Trapped Emotion

2. Resonance

3. Psychic Trauma

4. Despair Anchor[3]

5. Post Hypnotic Suggestion (PHS)

6. Incorrect Thought Pattern

7. Organ Imbalance

8. Heart Wall

Column B

1. Toxic Thought Energy

2. Broadcast Message

3. Limiting Belief [4]

4. Inherited Psychic Trauma

5. Thought Allergy

6. Saboteur

7. Image

8. Hidden Heart Wall

The Emotion Code™ Chart

	Column A	Column B
Row 1 Heart or Small Intestine	Abandonment Betrayal Forlorn Lost Love Unreceived	Effort Unreceived Heartache Insecurity Overjoy Vulnerability
Row 2 Spleen or Stomach	Anxiety Despair Disgust Nervousness Worry	Failure Helplessness Hopelessness Lack of Control Low Self-Esteem
Row 3 Lung or Colon	Crying Discouragement Rejection Sadness Sorrow	Confusion Defensiveness Grief Self-Abuse Stubborness
Row 4 Liver or Gall Bladder	Anger Bitterness Guilt Hatred Resentment	Depression Frustration Indecisiveness Panic Taken for Granted
Row 5 Kidneys or Bladder	Blaming Dread Fear Horror Peeved	Conflict Creative Insecurity Terror Unsupported Wishy Washy
Row 6 Glands & Sexual Organs	Humiliation Jealousy Longing Lust Overwhelm	Pride Shame Shock Unworthy Worthless

Emotion Code Heart-Wall Flowchart

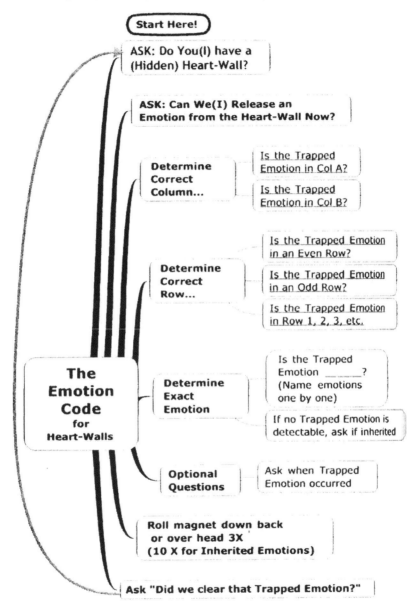

Start Here!

ASK: Do You(I) have a (Hidden) Heart-Wall?

ASK: Can We(I) Release an Emotion from the Heart-Wall Now?

Determine Correct Column...
- Is the Trapped Emotion in Col A?
- Is the Trapped Emotion in Col B?

Determine Correct Row...
- Is the Trapped Emotion in an Even Row?
- Is the Trapped Emotion in an Odd Row?
- Is the Trapped Emotion in Row 1, 2, 3, etc.

Determine Exact Emotion
- Is the Trapped Emotion _____? (Name emotions one by one)
- If no Trapped Emotion is detectable, ask if inherited

Optional Questions
- Ask when Trapped Emotion occurred

The Emotion Code for Heart-Walls

Roll magnet down back or over head 3X (10 X for Inherited Emotions)

Ask "Did we clear that Trapped Emotion?"

Follow the Heart-Wall flowchart above and the Chart of Emotions at the right to release Heart-Walls.

The Heart's Wall

Your heart is more than just the pump in your chest. There is reason to believe that it stores memories and that trapped emotions can be lodged there.[63] Biblically defined the heart is the mind, the will and the emotions. Thus our hearts are the core of who we are because it includes the way that we think. Christ said, "Out of the overflow of the heart the mouth speaks" (Matthew 12:34). And Proverbs 23:7 says, "As a man thinks in his heart, so is he." Our thoughts will determine our emotions and many people are emotionally driven and so we act upon those emotions that have been created by what we think about.

Our subconscious mind knows that it must protect the heart. In order to do this it can literally create a wall of energy around your heart to do so. We can make our heart walls of anything. When I had taken down the whole thing, the world really began to respond to me differently in very positive ways, even the first day! Many people who feel disconnected from others will find that their heart wall is keeping them from that connectedness. Our love-energy cannot find its way past our wall to get out. At the same time, the love of others cannot reach us because it does not penetrate our own hearts being blocked by our wall. Married couples may begin walling each other off and over time become distant and alienated from one another. If both had their heart walls taken down, then unity could conceivably be

---

63 This is a result of organ transplants wherein the recipients of the organs report that they now have the emotions that the donor had towards the same things.

regained. This can also be true in any and all relationships. If you have built a wall it can indeed come down.

To find out if someone has a heart wall simply ask. Unless you ask the person's subconscious mind if they have a heart wall, it will not reveal itself. If the initial answer comes back negative ask specifically if there is a hidden heart wall. I discovered, by writing this chapter, that I had cleared my heart wall, but that I still have a *hidden* heart wall to clear! I did not know that someone could have *both*. A hidden heart wall really is not a different type of heart wall but is simply more difficult to find.

Because these particular trapped emotions are no longer recognized as such, they are stone and mortar for a protective wall around the heart, you have to have the subconscious mind admit their existence or they cannot be cleared. Once the subconscious admits that they are trapped emotions it will be able to release them the same as it does all of the other trapped emotions. You will use the same process of asking the questions and narrowing down the chart to the specific emotions to be dismantled. Then clear them the same way.

We do not choose which emotions of the heart wall will be cleared or in what order. The subconscious mind does that by itself.

Some people's heart wall will be ready to clear in its entirety the first time and others will have to take it down brick by brick. But it will eventually come down when the person is ready.

One very important note is that unless someone is ready to let go of that protective wall, it needs to stay in place. That person's subconscious mind will know what is best, and when it is the right time to dismantle it. It may yet be serving a very important function and should remain in place.

If permission is granted then proceed until the body can go no further. Clear as much of it as the body is willing to let go of.

If you are wondering if you have a heart wall, ask yourself. If you feel that you cannot afford to let go of the wall, or if you feel that it is necessary to keep it in order to protect yourself, then please consider the cost long term of having heart walls. People around the world feel disconnected and lonely and live their lives for years, sometimes decades, without experiencing the joy that comes from having love penetrate their lives and the joy of loving others. The heart wall prevents the love-energy flow that everyone craves in their lives. Taking the wall down will allow love's energy to begin to flow in to you, and out from you. It may be a whole new experience of wholeness and connection that you have no recollection of experiencing. Your wall may have been in place for as long as you can even remember; there are children that have been born loaded down with toxic emotions (I am one of them) and some that have been born with heart walls. They lead ultimately only to alienation. Globally they lead to ethnic cleansing, racism, terrorism and wars. On a personal scale they devastate families and individual's lives. It is likely, for example, that the overwhelming majority of violent criminals have heart walls that insulate them from the injury of the violence that they perpetrate. The patterns of abuse that heart walls create is perpetuated from generation to generation. Since these toxic emotions can be inherited by others, it is possible that they have transferred from one generation to the next for a long time. This can now end. Let us be willing to be the individuals who will take the risk and be instrumental in healing ourselves, our families, our relationships and ultimately our world. Will you join me?

Another Word About Heart Walls

It is possible to have more than one heart wall. I have discovered 12 of them so far! Each has to be dismantled separately. I have had the general heart wall, a positive heart wall of happy or positive memories to wrap myself in and comfort myself. But I have found numerous others including a heart wall to wealth, a heart wall to God, a heart wall to society, to life and even one to love that was formed entirely *inutero*!! Slowly I am taking down these walls, except for the one made of loving memories. It does not want to be dismantled!! Be sure that you, too, find all of them for an abundant and fulfilling life!

Encoding Positive Thoughts

I have recently discovered that just as we are able to have toxic, negative and destructive thoughts take up residence in our thinking and control us we are able to encode into our thinking the positive thoughts. As the negatives are usually involuntary these are very deliberate. These positive thoughts can and should be what controls our thinking in place of the toxicities that have sabotaged us. Through the use of muscle testing I have come across 24 such categories and I have listed them below.

1. Empowering Beliefs

2. Encouraging Thoughts

3. Strengthening Belief

4. Hopeful Thought

5. Hopeful Belief

6. Virtuous Thoughts

7. Christlike Ambitions

8. Christlike Qualities

9. Virtuous Qualities

10. Obedient Thoughts

11. Freeing Thoughts

12. Peaceful Thoughts

13. Affirming Belief

14. Mental Empowerment

15. Positive Affirmations about God

16. Loving Thoughts

17. Freedom

18. The Vine & the Branches (Abiding)

19. Biblical Authority

20. Scriptural Beliefs

21. Beliefs that Free

22. Attitudes

23. Spiritual Empowerment

24. Emotion is Positive (sanctified emotions)

If you are interested in encoding something, like the qualities of love in 1 Corinthians 13, then ask your body, using muscle testing, if it would receive those encodings. If yes, narrow down the list to which category it would fall under. In this case, it is not surprising, that they would fall under Loving Thoughts.

Using positive intention again choose to encode "I am patient" or "I am kind", etc. Beware that if there is still too much toxicity inside of you it will not take; the body will reject it because it is yet a lie. You may have to wait until much later, after more processing of the toxins has taken place to encode the positives. Your body will know. Trust it.

Here are some other examples that I have found along the way:

Affirming Belief: I love God.

Christlike Quality: I can be tactful (love is not rude).

Obedient Thought: I can make my thoughts obedient.

Mental Empowerment: I can learn; I can learn anything.

Freeing Thought: I can concentrate fully.

Peaceful Thought: I have peace.

Believe it or not - and I do not know if it has made any difference! - my body was willing to encode the Empowering Thought "I release genius."

Just figure out what you want to encode and then ask your body if it will receive it and under what category. Having these thoughts, or thoughts like them, as the foundation of your thinking will greatly improve your life. It goes a step further than simply removing what sabotages your thinking and relationships. It is an actual step towards attaining victorious living. Join me!

Other Helpful Suggestions

This chapter is about other things that people can try that can, in some cases, greatly reduce or exacerbate PTSD symptoms. These are not medical counsel per se but constitute suggestions based upon my own experience and that of people that I know, or know of. Each of these should be considered separately and be chosen only after consulting a qualified medical practitioner.[64] Besides medical doctors, there are also qualified holistic health chiropractors, herbal remedy specialists, kinesiologists, iridologists, etc. These practitioners who are outside of the typical American Medical Association's (AMA) control may have plenty of good ideas that you will not hear from anyone licensed by the AMA. Please listen to them; they have been *the* solution for me personally and many others that I know.

Chiropractors

This can be a tremendous boost to your body's ability to recover from more than just a car accident. When I finally found an excellent chiropractor my spinal column was adjusted and became

---

64

straight, and my neck's curvature was greatly improved. Only about one-tenth of the chiropractors out there can actually produce these types of results so you have to look very carefully. A good "cracking" may be helpful but corrective chiropractic is another matter altogether. Look carefully and be discerning.

For more information please look at Revolution Chiropractic Wellness Center's website. www.revolution-chiropractic.com

Massage Therapy

Who doesn't like a good massage? This has been a marvelous tool for me because I have fibromyalgia. Besides moving the many toxins through the body, it also reduces pain, muscle tension and stress. If you have not tried a massage, then please do so. And if you do not like the first masseuse that you get, try another.

Herbal Remedies

This is questioned by many people and honestly, some claims are absolutely ridiculous. But many of these things do actually work. Using applied kinesiology you can find out if they will work for your body, and if they will work with other things that you are taking.

Please take the time to find a reputable herbalist before jumping in. Never begin a new regiment without proper medical guidance and applied kinesiology. This is very important. But there are simple things that work for many or most people and may be a good place to start. For example, the natural remedies melatonin and valerian are herbal sleep aids. They are non-addictive and can replace prescription sleep aids on some occasions (a combination of the two did this for me). There are also vitamins, organic oils, and teas, among other herbals.

The real value of this approach is that reputable organics do not come with the harmful side effects that prescription medicines invariably do. While they are not covered by insurance, they are far better for you in the long haul. The prescription medicines can have remarkably toxic side effects and do long term damage to organs and the body's overall health. Often times chronic conditions can be managed better with herbals than with prescriptions. Nevertheless, do not stop taking a prescription medicine without first contacting your pharmacist or doctor.

One other caution is noted: avoid online sources and those from out of the country. These remedies are not monitored by the FDA or any other reputable agency and therefore should not be trusted blindly. Please be sure that you only use companies producing products with a proven track record. Get personal recommendations from people you have consulted in person, or by trying one that is on the shelf first. The quality of these items is a significant matter.

Go Organic

This may be a cliché by now but it works. If you try it for a couple of weeks and do not notice anything different then you will not have lost a thing.

217

I watched friends of mine shift from processed food to organic and loose weight. So I tried it. It worked.

Many have also switched to organic cleaners. This, too, is good. As we take in less of the environment's harmful chemicals, we gradually detoxify our bodies. As we do so we feel better. Our moods can be uplifted, our sleeping improves, energy soars and so much more. Allergic sensitivities can also improve.

Another important issue under this heading is that processed foods have so many neurotoxins in them. The additives, preservatives, artificial sweeteners, monosodium glutamate, colors and so forth can accumulate in our bodies and be harmful to us. This is especially true for those with ADD/ ADHD and PTSD. I personally discovered upon discontinuing MSG, a known neurotoxin, that my violent thought tendencies diminished markedly. Upon accidentally consuming some after not having it for a period, I found that my violent and intrusive thoughts *skyrocketed*. Again, I went ahead and discontinued it and improved. But it takes time for these toxins to metabolize out of our systems, and the process can feel like it takes forever.

I realize that the cost of organic food is high, especially compared to the processed stuff that lower income people consume. But the benefits can soon outweigh our costs financially. Furthermore, the health benefit of weight loss alone can be substantial.

Another note here is that these healthy foods will help keep blood sugar within good tolerances and this helps keep our moods stable and aids in sleeping better. When I was diagnosed with hyperglycemia (low blood sugar) I was informed that one of the challenges that it poses is the nightmares that low blood sugar induces. If this is stabilized, however, this problem is eliminated in our already challenged sleep patterns (or lack thereof). When sleep is so difficult to get in the first place, as it is for those with PTSD, anything we can do to make this better is a plus.

Cleanses

There are many herbal cleanses for your body. Again, please use only reputable cleanses as they could potentially be harmful if they are low-grade or conflict with other things that you are taking.

I have personally done a gallbladder flush three times with significant results, including the elimination of parasites from taking care of a rescue animal. The parasites would never have been discovered by the AMA's professionals but the chiropractor's herbalist found them and I was able to destroy them by using a topical oil for 30 days. No harmful side effects but tremendous results!

I also tried a digestive track cleanse when I first started that was far too harsh for me and caused dark blood to be eliminated in my stools. Clearly it was the wrong cleanse for me (it has not been tested using kinesiology and I had not yet heard of that tool to test it myself). Beware!

Almost anyone who has been taking prescription medications or eating processed food will need to do whole body cleanses to process out all of the harmful toxins. And many of us will need to do a heavy metal or lead cleanse, despite the fact that lead is not in many substances any longer (unless from China).

Prayer

This may sound ridiculous, but I can personally testify, as can countless others, that the mind can calm itself and focus better after seeking the Lord in prayer. In fact, if I go without prayer for a day I notice that my thoughts and emotions are no longer sanctified and I can overreact and emotionally get out of whack with what is pleasing to God.

A word of caution: eastern meditation is the absence of thought whereas biblical meditation is to think on the Words of God. Eastern meditation takes down the mental defenses necessary to defend us against the world's vain philosophies and demonic spirits. This makes us vulnerable to demonic possession. This cannot happen when meditating upon the Words of God from Scripture. Memorizing verses and hymns can keep our minds on more pleasant matters when the wrong thoughts come to us. Capturing the thoughts and making them subject to our wills is a learning process but very critical in overcoming the thought habits that destroy us, especially in PTSD.

Give it a try. Ask Christ to forgive you and indwell you and begin communicating with Him regularly and faithfully and see what happens. As you imbed the Words of God on your sinful heart you become transformed from the inside out.

Exercise

Enough good cannot be said about the benefits of moving your body. Taking walks, stretching, and swimming (are usually good enough for most people). Whatever form the exercise takes, it helps relieve depression, burns calories, gives muscle tone and generally increases health. While you may wish to consult your doctor about what specific exercises you should do or not do, it is unlikely that any doctor would tell you to be sedentary.

Detoxification Baths

Here is another item that can really help you feel better. Detoxification baths remove bodily wastes that are still in the blood stream and need to be processed out through the excretory pathways (urine and colon). These baths can short-circuit their course and pull them out through the skin thereby relieving the kidneys and liver from the need to process them.

Epsom salts are one organic method of detoxifying. However, the most effective one that I personally know of is apple cider vinegar. If you use half of a gallon to a gallon of cider vinegar in as hot of water as you can bear for 30-45 minutes, soaking the affected areas specifically (possibly having to lie down in the tub), you will feel a noticeable decrease in the pain and stiffness in those areas.

I try to use this approach at least once a week due to fibromyalgia. It reduces muscle pain, and if done before going to bed, it can promote relaxation and better rest. It is helpful for colds and flu bugs to be drawn out of the body, too.

There are also other bath salts and you may freely experiment with what is available. Typically the organic ones will be best, as the products are not adding more environmental toxins to your body to process after the bath is over.

If you do not like the aroma of a particular product, it is probably best if you do not use it. Your body's response indicates whether or not it would work for your chemistry. If your mind responds favorably or very favorably to a particular scent when inhaled deeply then use that one because it goes well with your body chemistry. Always listen to your body's response.

Oils

After I discovered something that astounded me I have opted to include this as a separate heading. Someone sent me a link to information regarding sage oil and its benefits in helping the energy during emotion code processing.[65] When I realized that my body had already asked for sage oil to be used during a massage in which I was processing I decided I was onto something. Upon inquiring of my body about it my body gave a very positive response to wanting the sage oil for processing! Interestingly, it also wants others, like lime, emotion, quiet scent, etc. I have found that using them really decreases the fatigue that I

---

65 http://hubpages.com/hub/Sage-essential-oil-uses-and-benefits

experience while processing and I generally feel less drained and even sometimes more energetic.

Given the fact that healing the body from traumatic emotions, traumatic events and toxic thoughts seems to take as much healing effort as healing from physical wounds and even surgery it makes sense to boost its healing energies and efforts in any way that would be conducive to that activity. Again, organic products matter, as do the quality of them. Be very wary of what sources you use as some are simply watered down and barely effect. They are not worth the money. If you hold the item in your hand and ask your body if it is a good quality item it will answer you with a yes or a no. Trust its response and go with it. Quality costs something. All medicine does.

While these oils are not essential to your processing they surely do enhance the effort! Use them if possible. And be sure to hold them altogether and ask if they will have a positive synergy or if you should avoid using one or two of them together. It is conceivable that you need to space two positive-acting substances some hours apart for maximum benefit.

Bibliography
For Nouthetic Approach To Ptsd

One purpose of this bibliography is to share a multitude of materials that many will never have known were available. The typical book store will not carry anything genuinely biblical nor indepth in the so-called "Christian Section" of the store. This list is intended to help those not familiar with biblical materials become aware of a few that the average reader will not have been exposed to. While not all of the materials in this listing are biblical in approach, and the author cannot recommend all of them equally, it is hoped that by including this variety of perspectives and resources the reader will be able to critically evaluate them on an individual basis.

Adams, Jay. *The Biblical View of Self-Esteem, Self-Love, Self-Image.* Harvest House Publishers, Eugene, OR: 1960.

Adams, Jay. *The Christian Counselor's Manual. The Practice of Nouthetic Counseling.* Zondervan Publishing, Grand Rapids, MI: 1973.

Adams, Jay. *Competent to Counsel. Introduction to Nouthetic Counseling.* Zondervan Publishing House, Grand Rapids, MI: 1970.

Adams, Jay. *From Forgiven to Forgiving.* Calvary Press, Amityville, NY: 1994.

Adams, Jay. *How to Handle Trouble.* Presbyterian and Reformed Publishing Co., Phillipsburg, NJ: 1982.

Adams, Jay. *How to Help People Change. The Four-Step Biblical Process.* Zondervan Publishing House, Grand Rapids, MI: 1986.

Adams, Jay. *How to Overcome Evil.* Presbyterian and Reformed Publishing Co., Phillipsburg, NJ: 1977.

Adams, Jay. *A Theology of Christian Counseling.* Zondervan Publishing House, Grand Rapids, MI: 1979.

Anderson, Taffy. *Treasures in Darkness. A Doctor's Personal Journey through Breast Cancer.* Moody Publishers, Chicago, IL: 2007.

Appel, John and Beebe, Gilbert. *Preventative Psychiatry: An Epidemiological Approach.* Journal of the American Medical Association, Vol. 131 (August 18, 1946).

Arthur, Kay. *Lord, Where are You When Bad Things Happen?* Waterbrook Press, Colorado Springs, CO: 1992.

Black, Jeffrey S. *Suicide. Understanding & Intervening.* Presbyterian and Reformed Publishing Co., Phillipsburg, NJ: 2003.

Bridges, Jerry. *Trusting God.* NavPress, Colorado Springs, CO: 1988.

Bristol, Goldie. *When It's Hard to Forgive.* Victor Books, Wheaton, IL: 1984.

Butterworth, Bill & Merrill, Dean. *The Promise of the Second Wind. It's Never Too Late to Pursue God's Best.* Water Brook Press, Colorado Springs, CO: 2003.

Clark, Jayne V. *Loneliness.* Punch Press, Winston-Salem, NC: 2005.

Coleman, Penny. *Flashback: Posttraumatic Stress Disorder, Suicide, & the Lessons of War.* Beacon Press, Boston, MA: 2006.

DeHaan, Martin. *The Forgiveness of God.* RBC Ministries, Grand Rapids, MI.

DeHaan, Martin. *How Much Does God Control?* RBC Ministries, Grand Rapids, MI.

DeMoss, Nancy Leigh. *Lies Women Believe & the Truth that Sets Them Free.* Moody Press, Chicago, IL: 2001.

Elliot, Elisabeth. *On Asking God Why and Other Reflections on Trusting God in a Twisted World.* Fleming H. Revell, Grand Rapids, MI: 1998.

Elliot, Elisabeth. *The Path of Loneliness. It May Seem a Wilderness, but it can Lead You to God.* Thomas Nelson Publishers, Nashville, TN: 1988.

Elliot, Elisabeth. *The Path Through Suffering. Discovering the Relationship Between God's Mercy and our Pain.* Servant Publications, Ann Arbor, MI: 1990.

Emlet, Michael R. *Chronic Pain. Living by Faith When Your Body Hurts.* New Growth Press, Greensboro, NC: 2010.

Evans, Patricia. *The Verbally Abusive Relationship. How to Recognize it and How to Respond.* _Adams Media Corporation, Avon, MA: 1996.

Feinberg, John. *Deceived By God? A Journey Through Suffering.* Crossway Books, Wheaton, IL: 1997.

Fitzpatrick, Elyse & Cornish, Carol. *Women Helping Women. A Biblical Guide to the Major Issues Women Face.* Harvest House Publishers, Eugene, OR: 1997.

Fitzpatrick, Elyse & Hendrickson, Laura. *Will Medicine Stop the Pain? Finding God's Healing for Depression, Anxiety & Other Troubling Emotions.* Moody Publishers, Chicago, IL: 2006.

George, Elizabeth. *Loving God with all Your Mind.* Harvest House Publishers, Eugene, OR: 1994.

Grinker, Roy, and Speigel, John. *Men Under Stress.* Irvington, New York, NY: 1979.

Ginsburg, Phil. *Deeper Still: For Those Who Grieve.* IBS Publishing, Colorado Springs, CO: 1997.

Herman, Judith. *Trauma and Recovery.* Basic Books Publisher, New York, NY: 1997.

Hutchcraft, Ron. *Surviving the Storms of Stress.* Discovery House Publishers, Grand Rapids, MI: 2000.

Ingram, Chip & Johnson, Becca. *Overcoming Emotions that Destroy. Practical Help for those Angry Feelings that Ruin Relationships.* BakerBooks, Grand Rapids, MI: 2009.

Jackson, Tim. *When Anger Burns.* Discovery House Publishers, Grand Rapids, MI: 1994.

Jackson, Tim. *When the Pain Won't Go Away. Dealing with the Aftereffects of Abortion.* Discovery House Publishers, Grand Rapids, MI.

Jackson, Tim. *When Forgiveness Seems Impossible.* Discovery House Publishers, Grand Rapids, MI: 1994.

Jaynes, Sharon. *Your Scars are Beautiful to God.* Harvest House Publishers, Eugene, OR: 2006.

Jones, Robert D. *Bad Memories. Getting Past Your Past.* Presbyterian and Reformed Publishers, Phillipsburg, NJ: 2004.

Jones, Robert D. *Freedom from Resentment. Stopping Hurts from Turning Bitter.* Presbyterian and Reformed Publishers, Phillipsburg, NJ: 2010.

Johnston, J. Kirk. *When Christians Sin. Restoring Wayward Christians.* Discovery House Publishers, Grand Rapids, MI: 1993.

Leman, Kevin & Carlson, Randy. *Unlocking the Secrets of Your Childhood Memories.* Thomas Nelson Publishers, Nashville, TN: 1989.

Lutzer, Erwin. *Putting Your Past Behind You. Finding Hope for Life's Deepest Hurts.* Moody Press, Chicago, IL: 1997.

MacArthur, John & Mack, Wayne. *Introduction to Biblical Counseling. A Basic Guide to the Principles and Practice of Counseling.* Word Publishing, Dallas, TX: 1994.

Maltz, Wendy. *The Sexual Healing Journey. A Guide for Survivors of Sexual Abuse.* Harpers Collins Publishers, New York, NY: 1991.

Miller, Alice. *Banished Knowledge. Facing Childhood Injuries.* Doubleday, Auckland, Germany: 1990.

Moore, Beth. *Breaking Free. Making Liberty in Christ a Reality in Life.* Broadman & Holman Publishers, Nashville, TN: 2000.

Moore, Beth. *Praying God's Word. Breaking Free From Spiritual Strongholds.* Broadman & Holman Publishers, Nashville, TN: 2003.

O'Connell, Kathleen. *Bruised By Life? Turn Life's Wounds into Gifts.* Deaconess Press, Minneapolis, MN: 1994.

Olson, Jeff. *When We Don't Measure Up. Escaping the Grip of Guilt.* Discovery House Publishers, Grand Rapids, MI: 1997.

Powlison, David. *God as Father. When Your Own Father Failed.* Punch Press, Winston-Salem, NC: 2004.

Powlison, David. *Grieving a Suicide. Help for the Aftershock.* New Growth Press, Greensboro, NC: 2010.

Powlison, David. *I Just Want to Die. Replacing Suicidal Thoughts with Hope.* New Growth Press, Greensboro, NC: 2010.

Powlison, David. *I'm Exhausted. What to Do When You're Always Tired.* New Growth Press, Greensboro, NC: 2010.

Powlison, David. *Sexual Assault. Healing Steps for Victims.* New Growth Press, Greensboro, NC: 2010.

Powlison, David. *Speaking Truth in Love: Counsel in Community.* New Growth Press, Greensboror, NC: 2005.

Powlison, David. *Why Me? Comfort for the Victimized.* Presbyterian and Reformed Publishers, Phillipsburg, NJ: 2003.

Presson, Ramon. *When Will My Life Not Suck? Authentic Hope for the Disillusioned.* New Growth Press, Greensboro, NC: 2011.

Sande, Ken. *The Peacemaker. A Biblical Guide to Resolving Personal Conflict.* Baker Books, Grand Rapids, MI: 2004.

Scott, Stuart. *The Exemplary Husband. A Biblical Perspective.* Focus Publishing, Bemidji, MN: 2000.

Tripp, Paul David. *Instruments in the Redeemer's Hands. People in Need of Change Helping People in Need of Change.* Presbyterian and Reformed Publishing, Phillipsburg, NJ: 2002.

Tripp, Paul David. *Suffering. Eternity Makes a Difference.* Presbyterian & Reformed Publishing, Phillipsburg, NJ: 2001.

Tripp, Paul David. *War of Words. Getting to the Heart of Your Communication Struggles.* Presbyterian and Reformed Publishers, Phillipsburg, NJ: 2000.

Welch, Edward. *Bipolar Disorder. Understanding and Help for Extreme Mood Swings.* New Growth Press, Greensboro, NC: 2010.

Welch, Edward. *Blame it on the Brain? Distinguishing Chemical Imbalances, Brain Disorders and Disobedience.* Presbyterian and Reformed Publishers, Phillipsburg, NJ: 1998.

Welch, Edward. *Depression: A Stubborn Darkness. Light for the Path.* Punch Press, Winston-Salem, NC: 2004.

Welch, Edward. *Depression. The Way Up When You are Down.* Presbyterian and Reformed Publishers, Phillipsburg, NJ: 2000.

Wilkinson, Bruce. *Secrets of the Vine. Breaking Through to Abundance.* Multnomah Publishers, Sisters, OR: 2001.

No Author Cited Pamphlets

Ten Reasons to Believe in Christ Rather Than Religion. Discovery House Publishers, Grand Rapids, MI: 1993.

Ten Reasons to Believe Christ Rose From the Dead. Discovery House Publishers, Grand Rapids, MI: 1993.

Ten Reasons to Believe in the Christian Faith. Discovery House Publishers, Grand Rapids, MI: 1993.

Ten Reasons to Believe in a God Who Allows Suffering. Discovery House Publishers, Grand Rapids, MI: 1993.

Made in the USA
Charleston, SC
30 December 2011